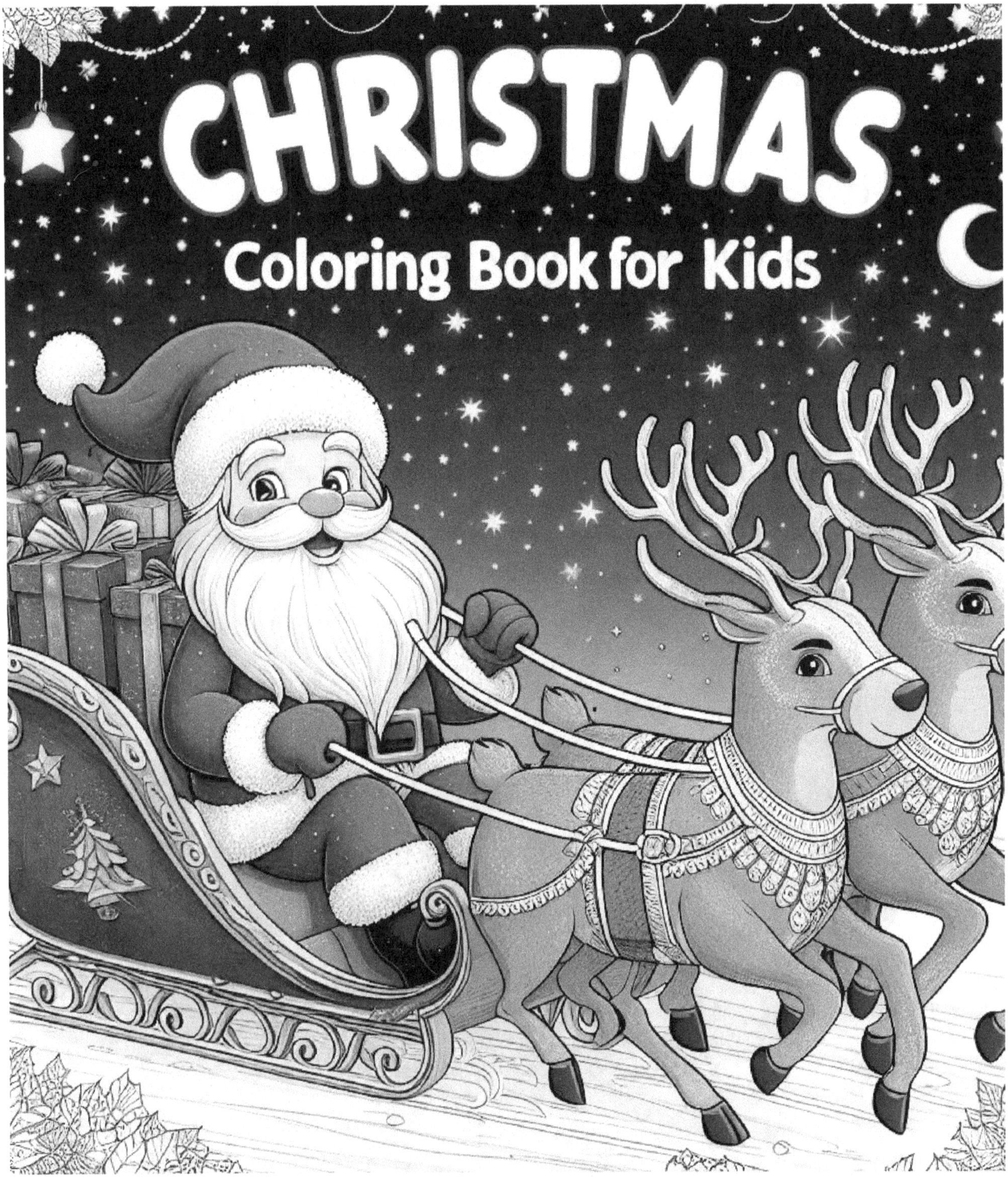

CHRISTMAS
Coloring Book for Kids

SIM EDITOR

We love receiving reviews from our customers.
If you have the opportunity to rate this notebook and make a review on Amazon, we will thank you for life.

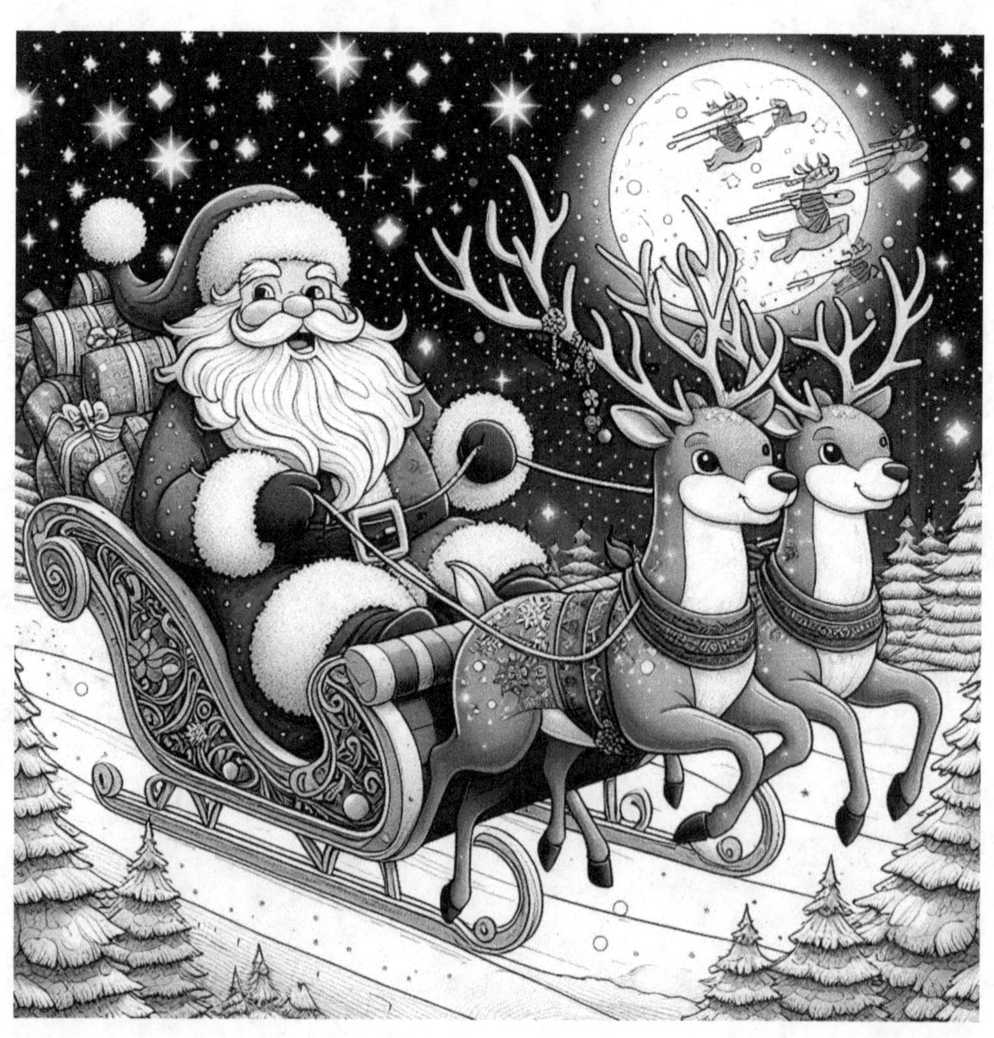

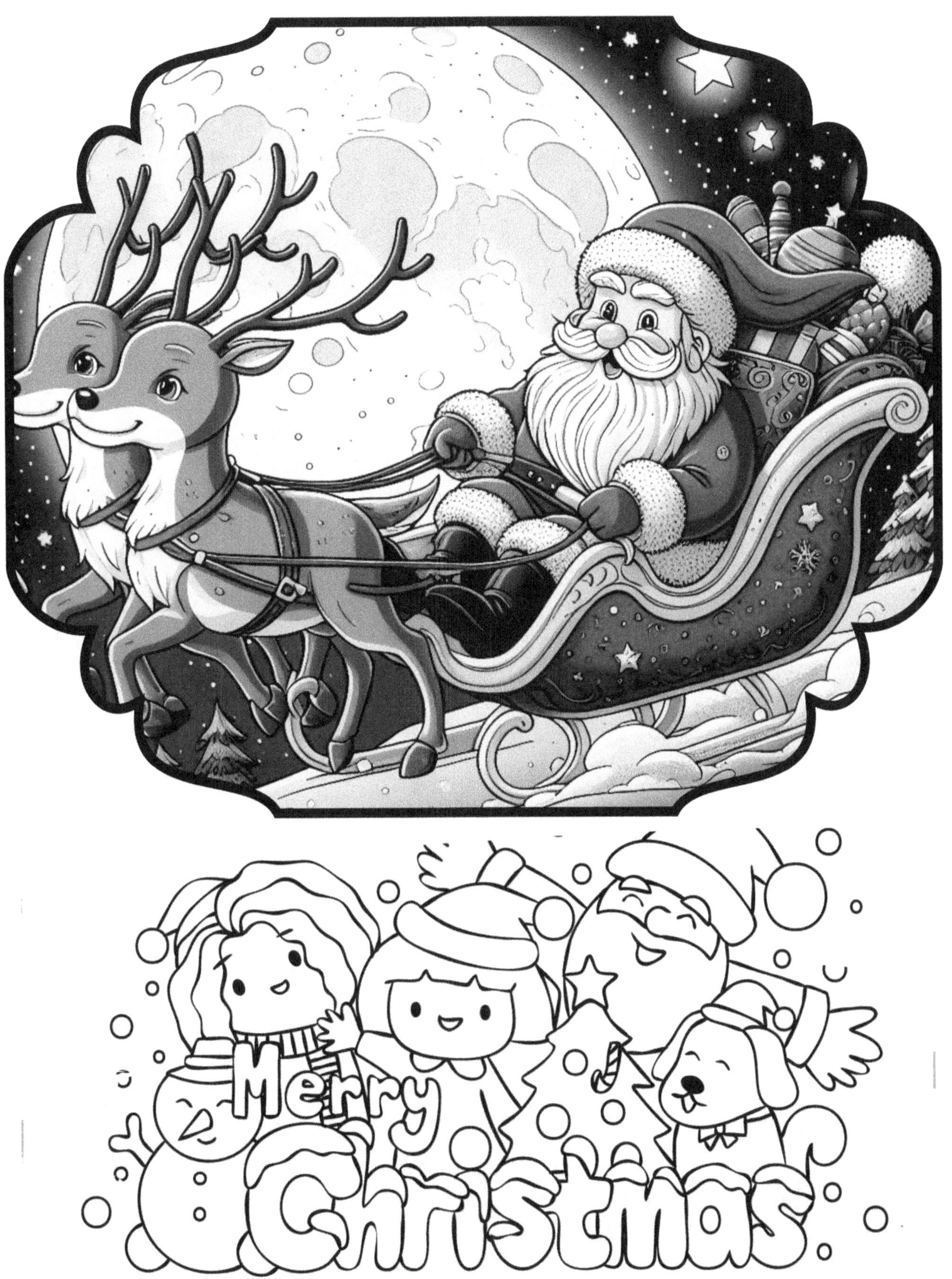
Merry
Christmas

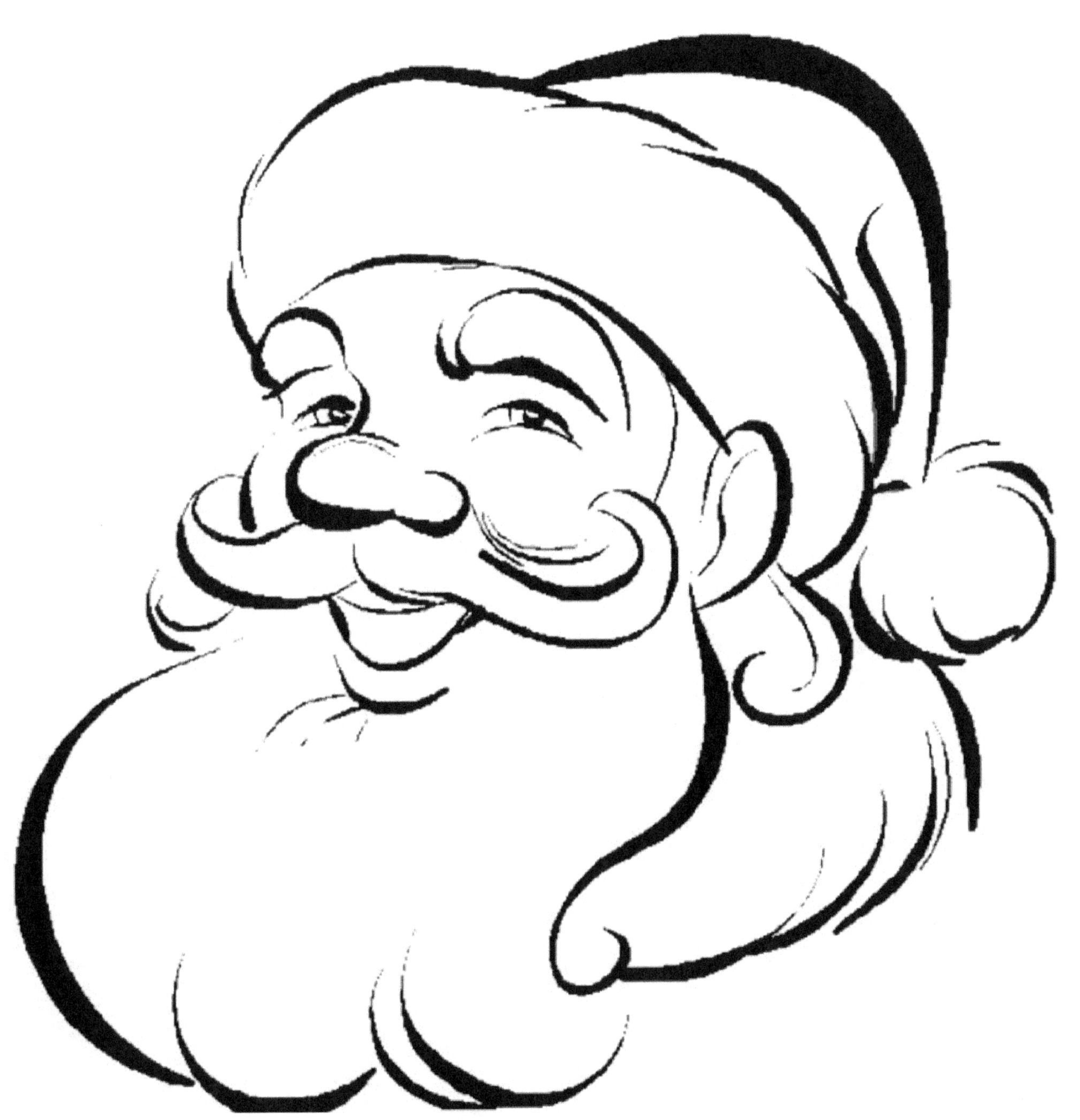

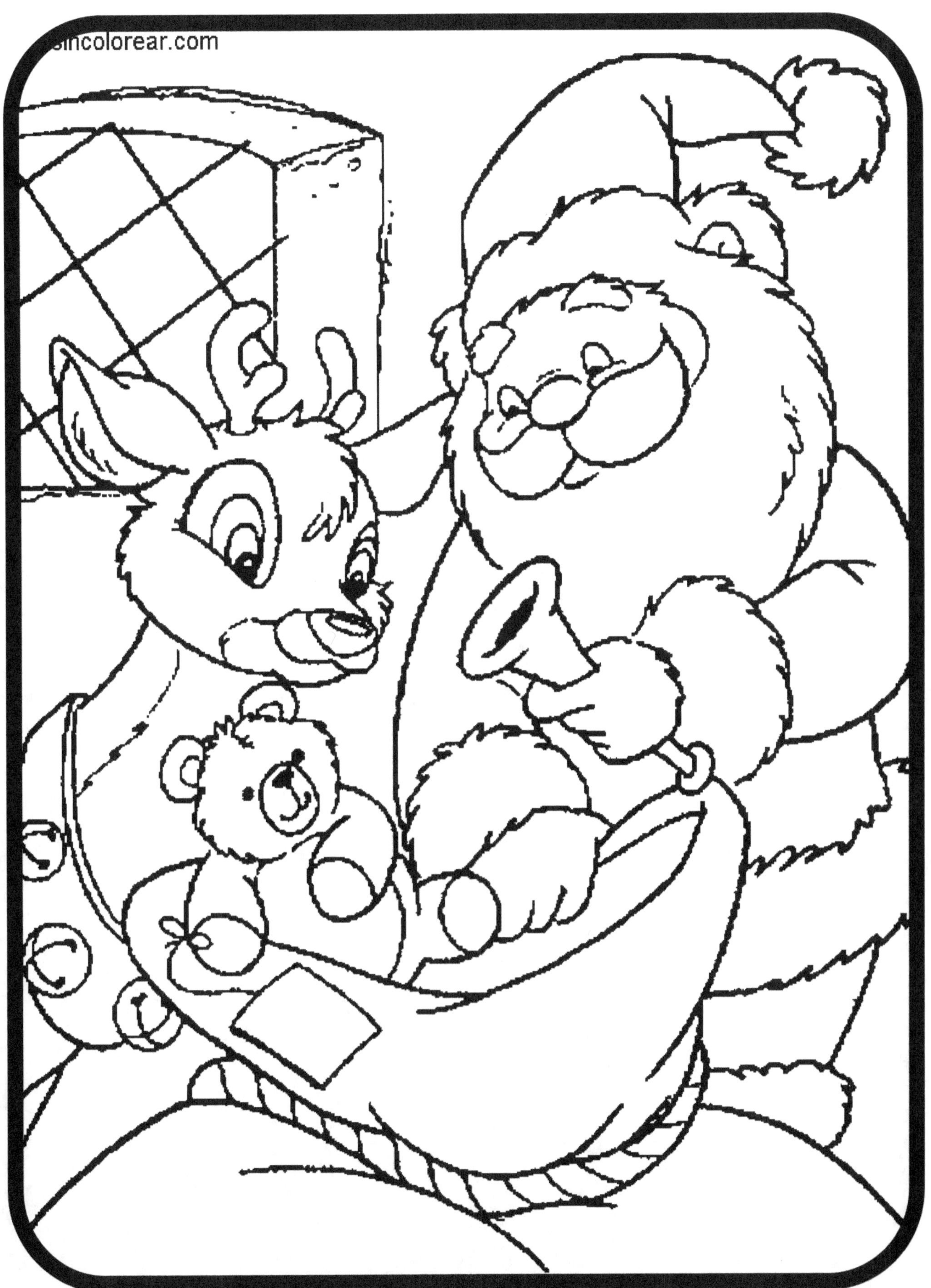
sincolorear.com

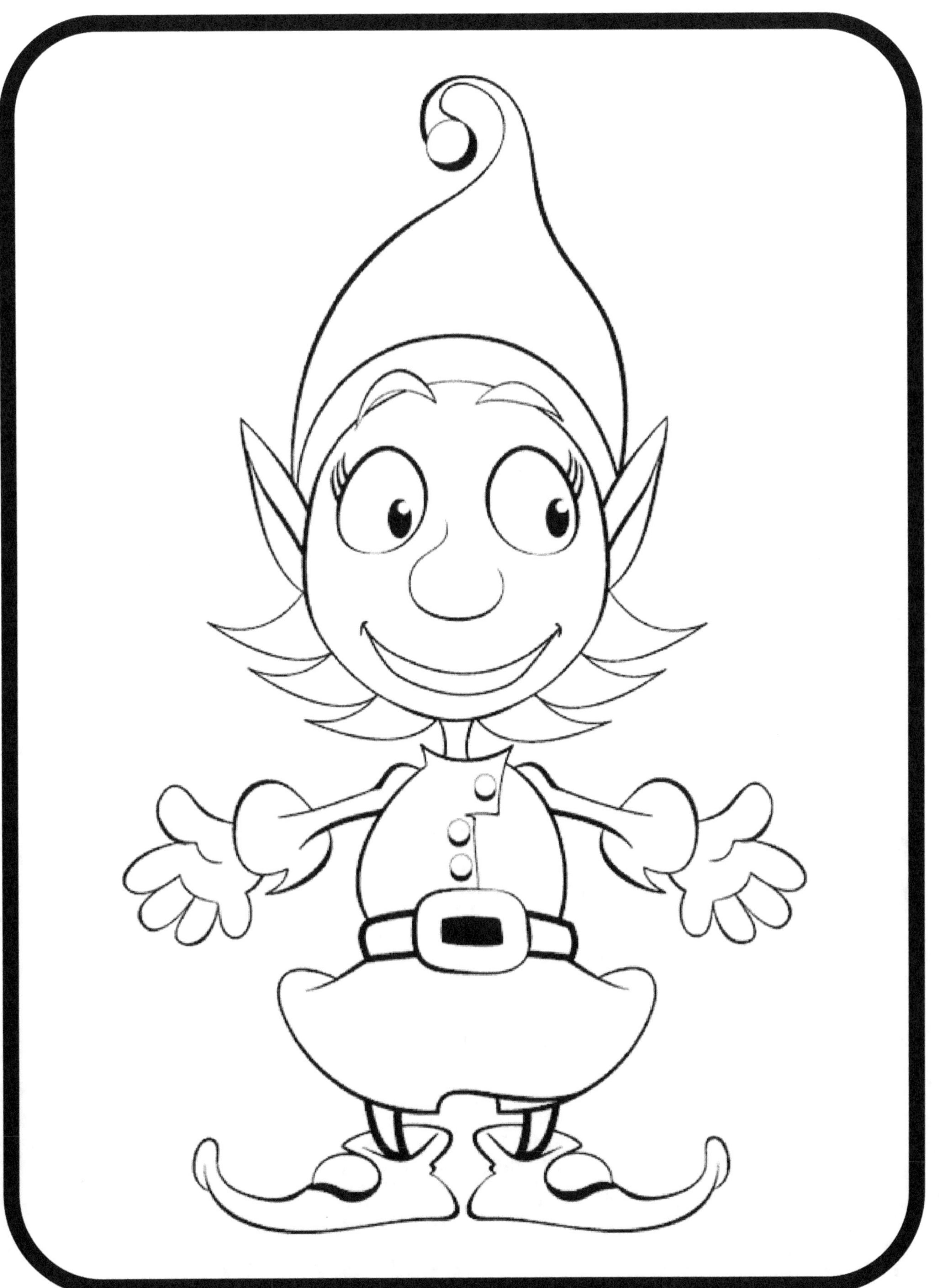

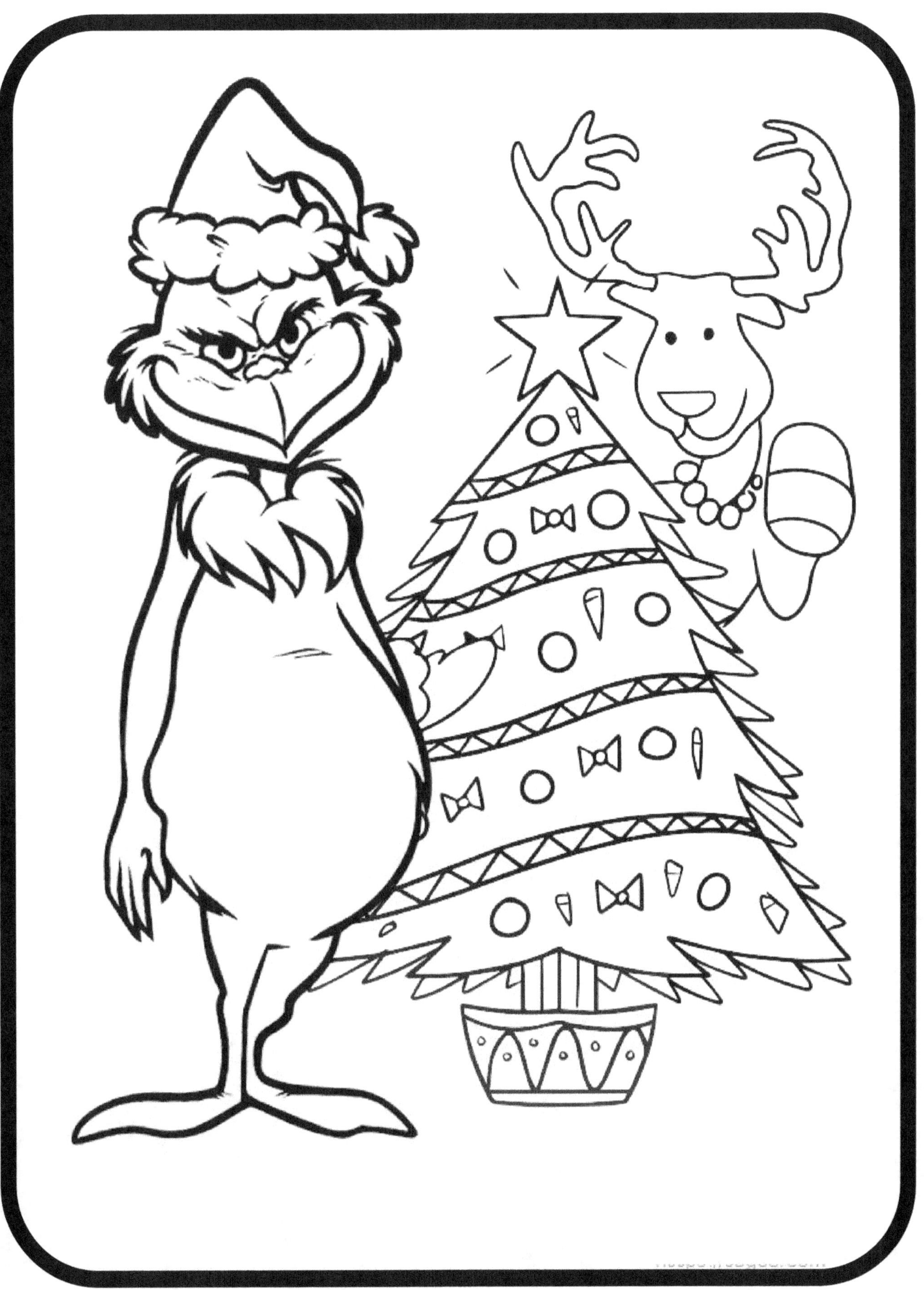

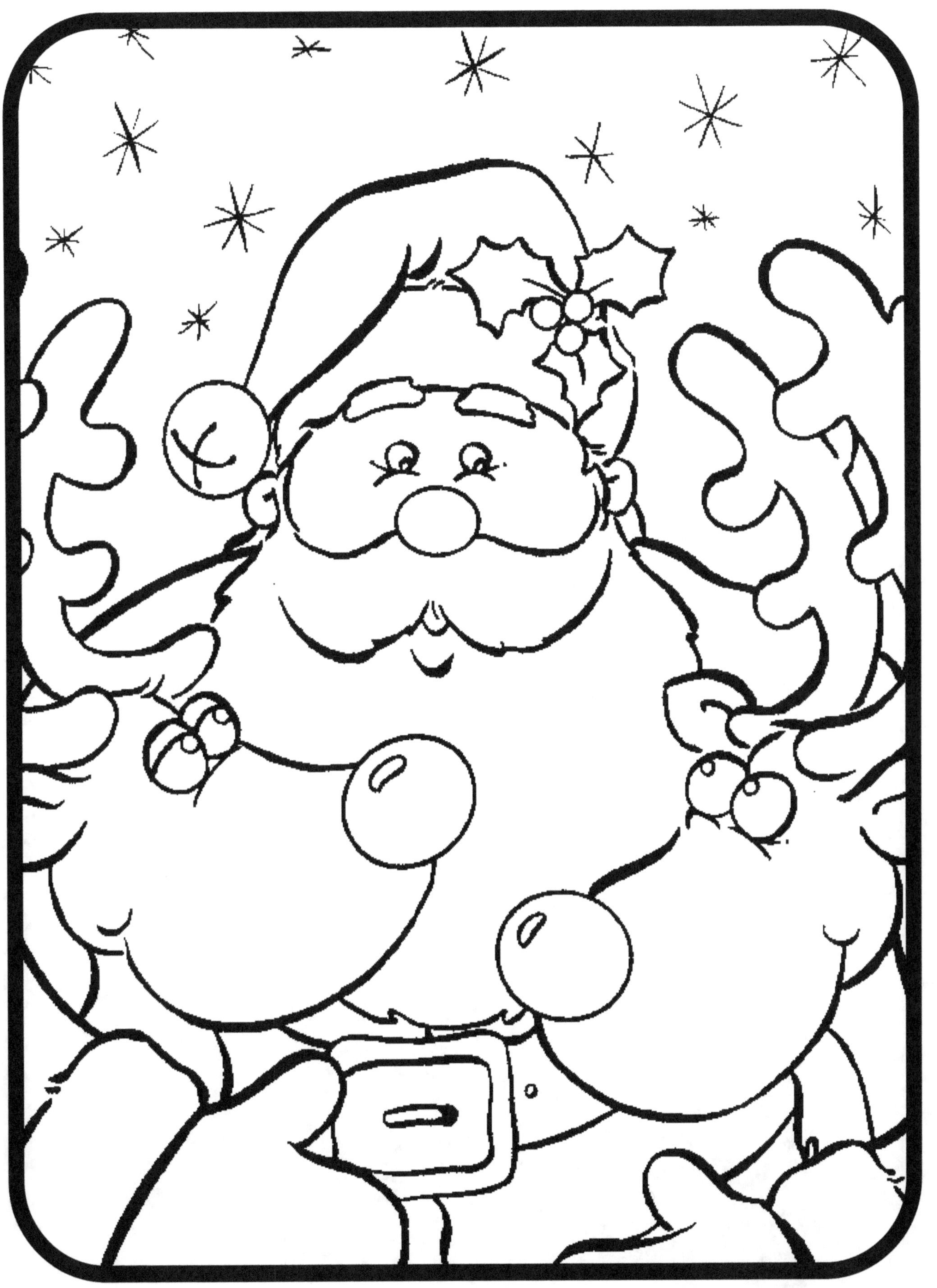

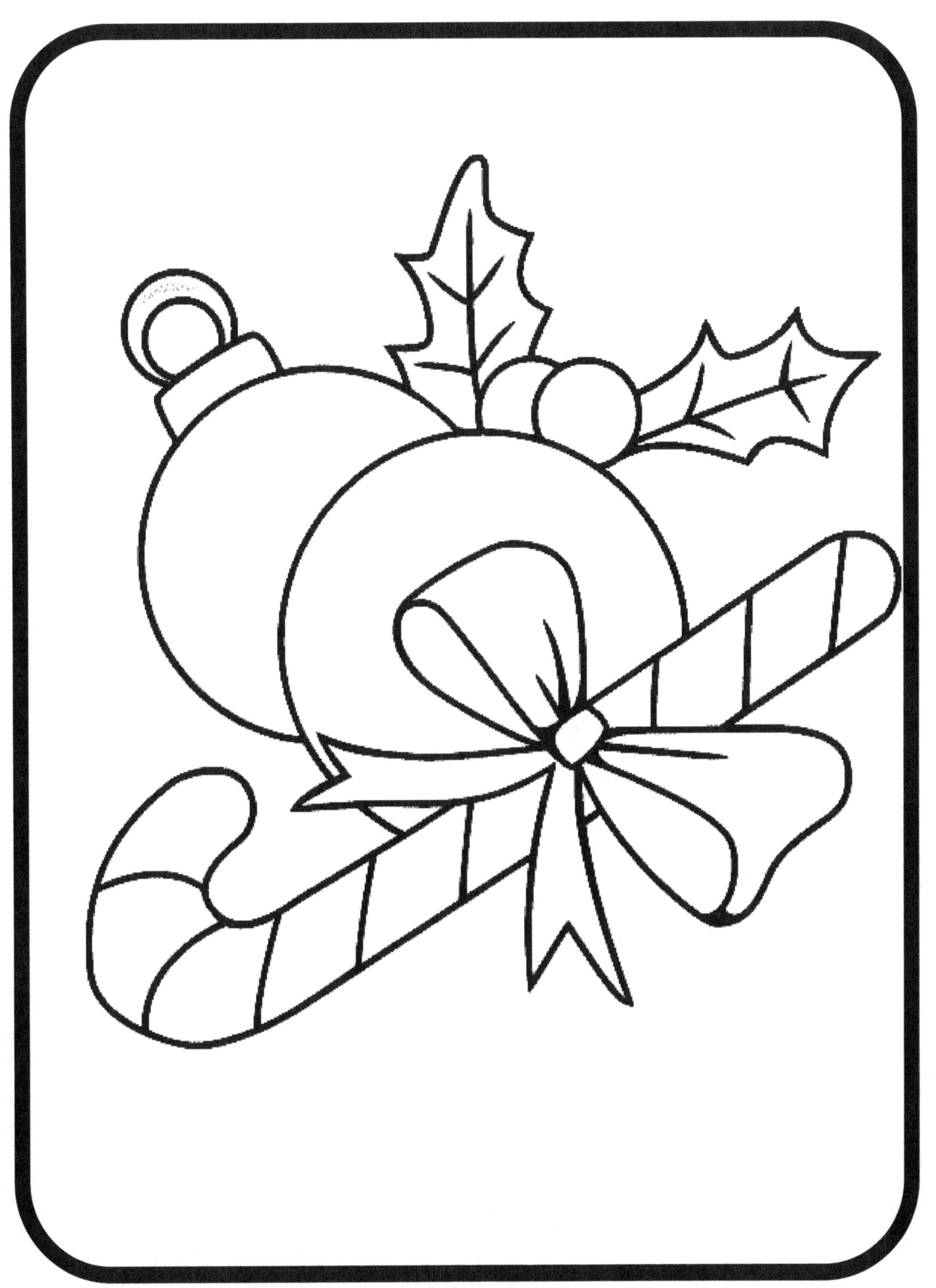

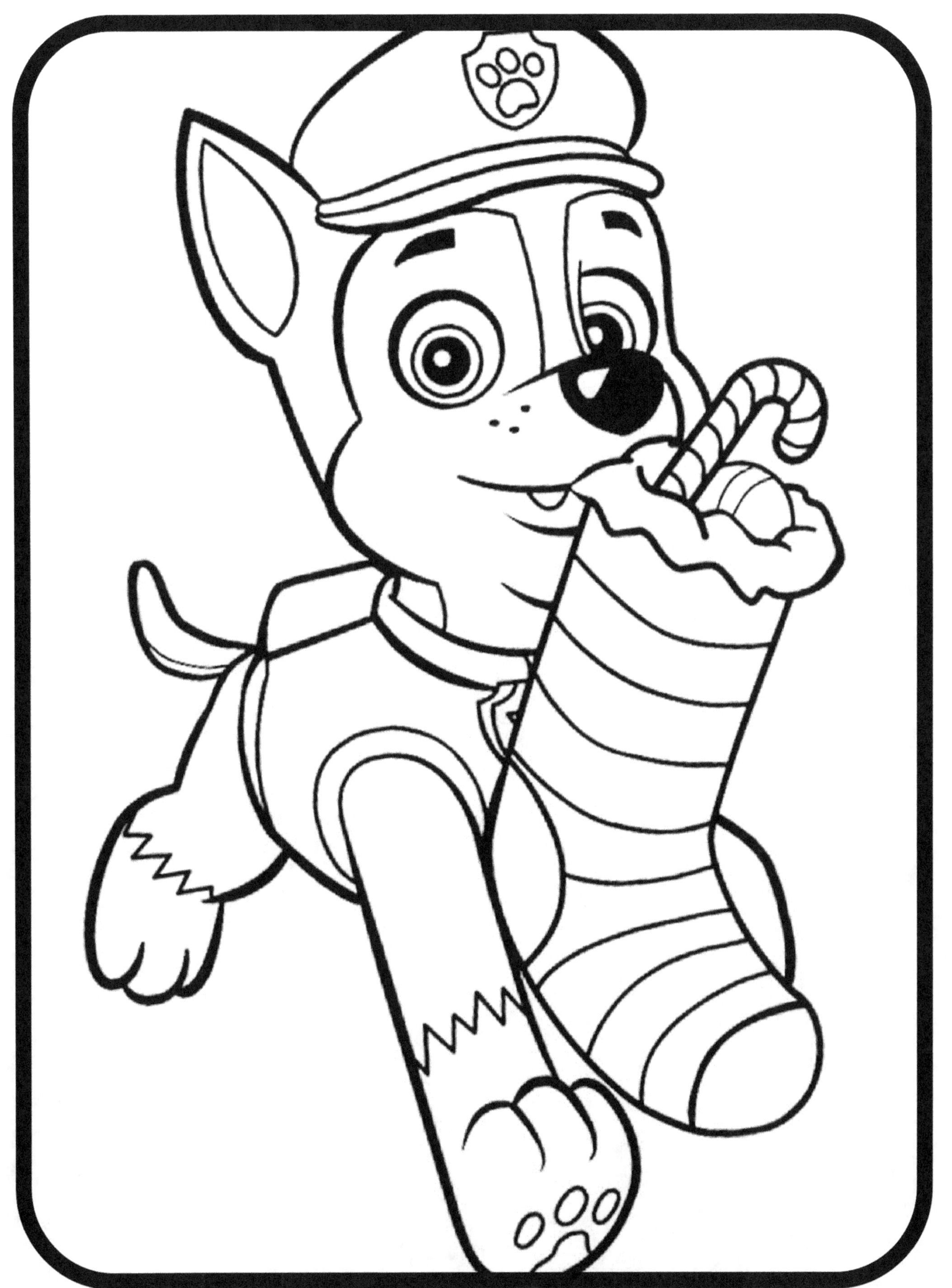

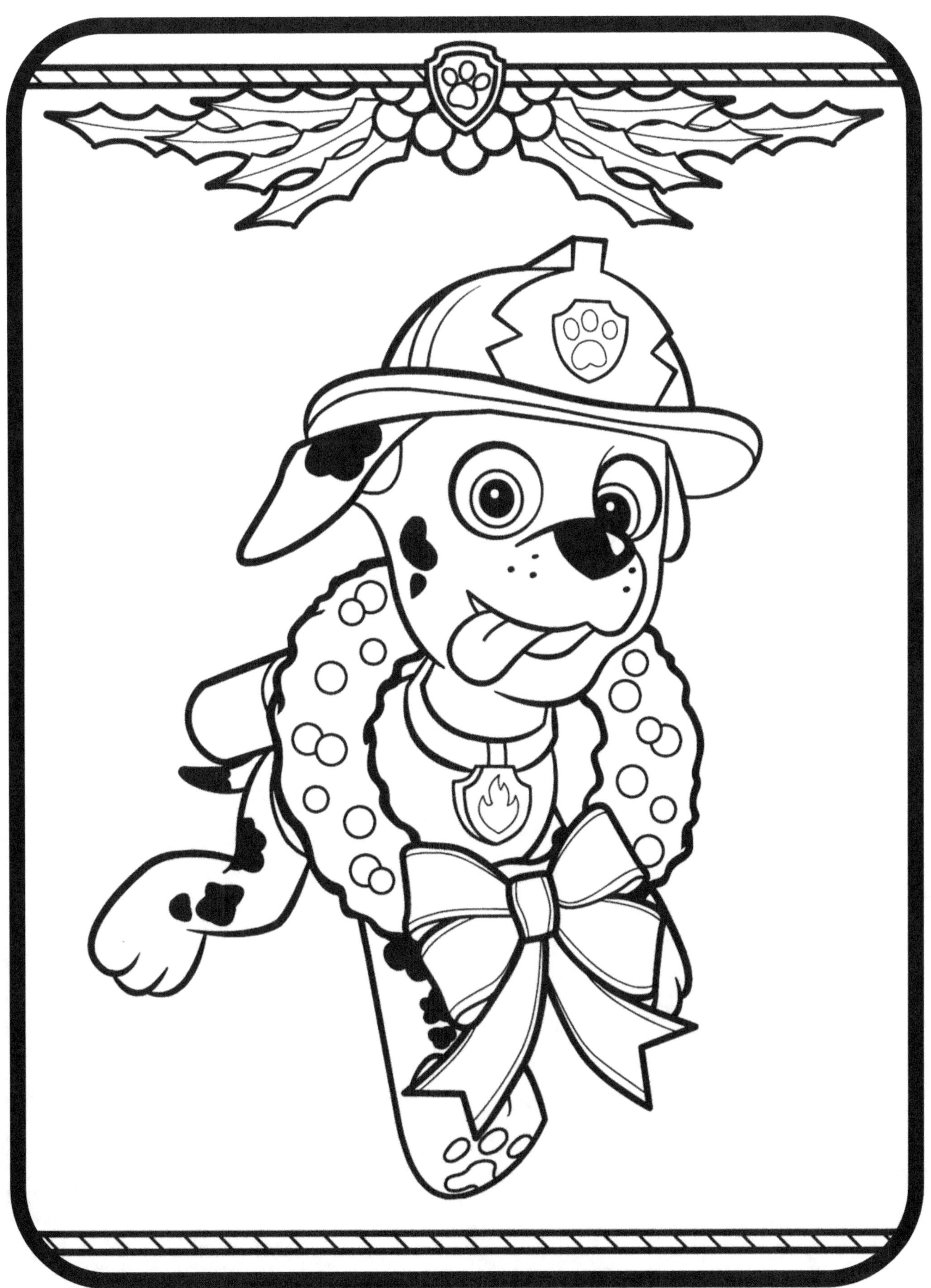

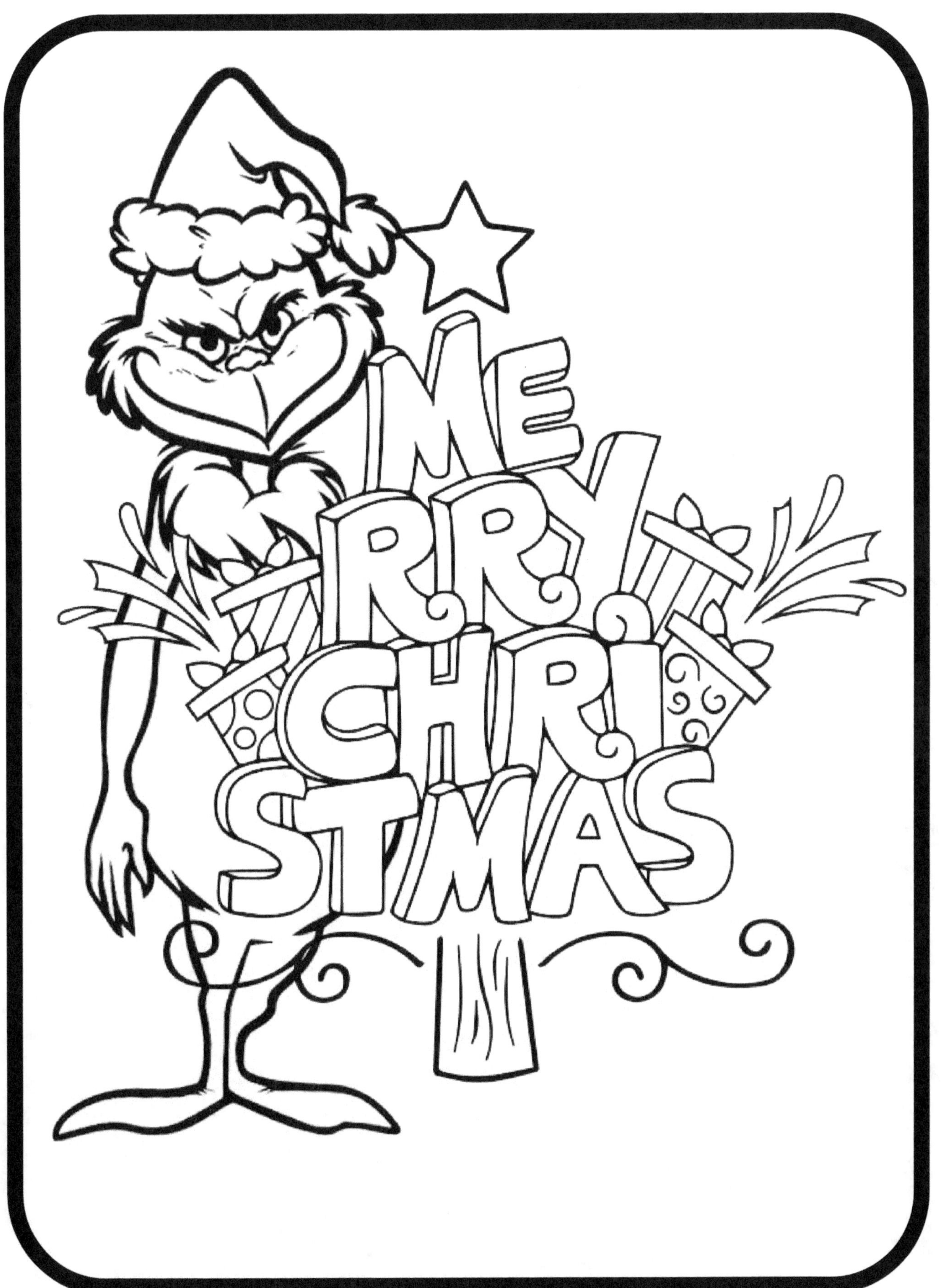

MERRY
CHRISTMAS

merry CHRISTMAS

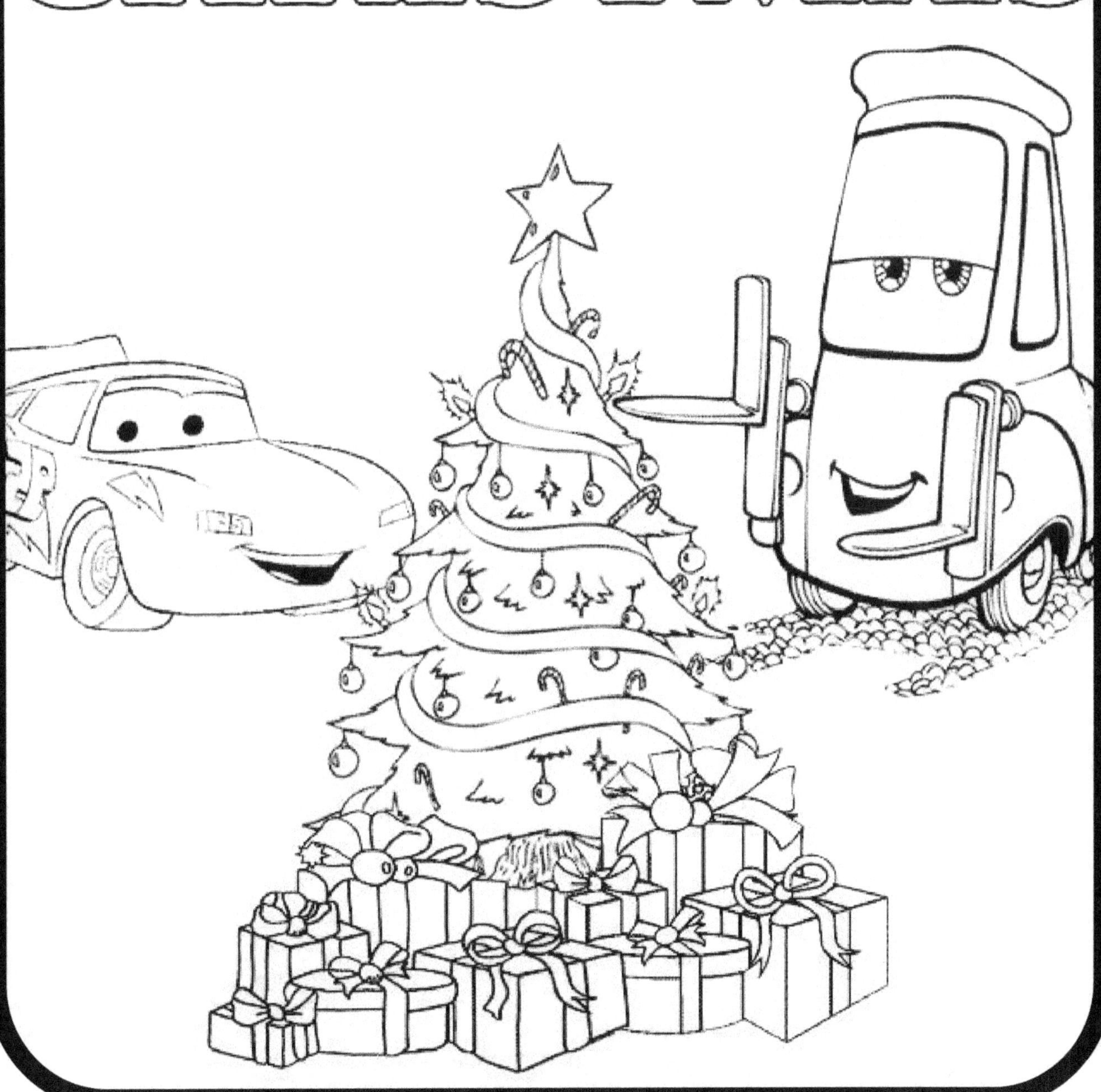

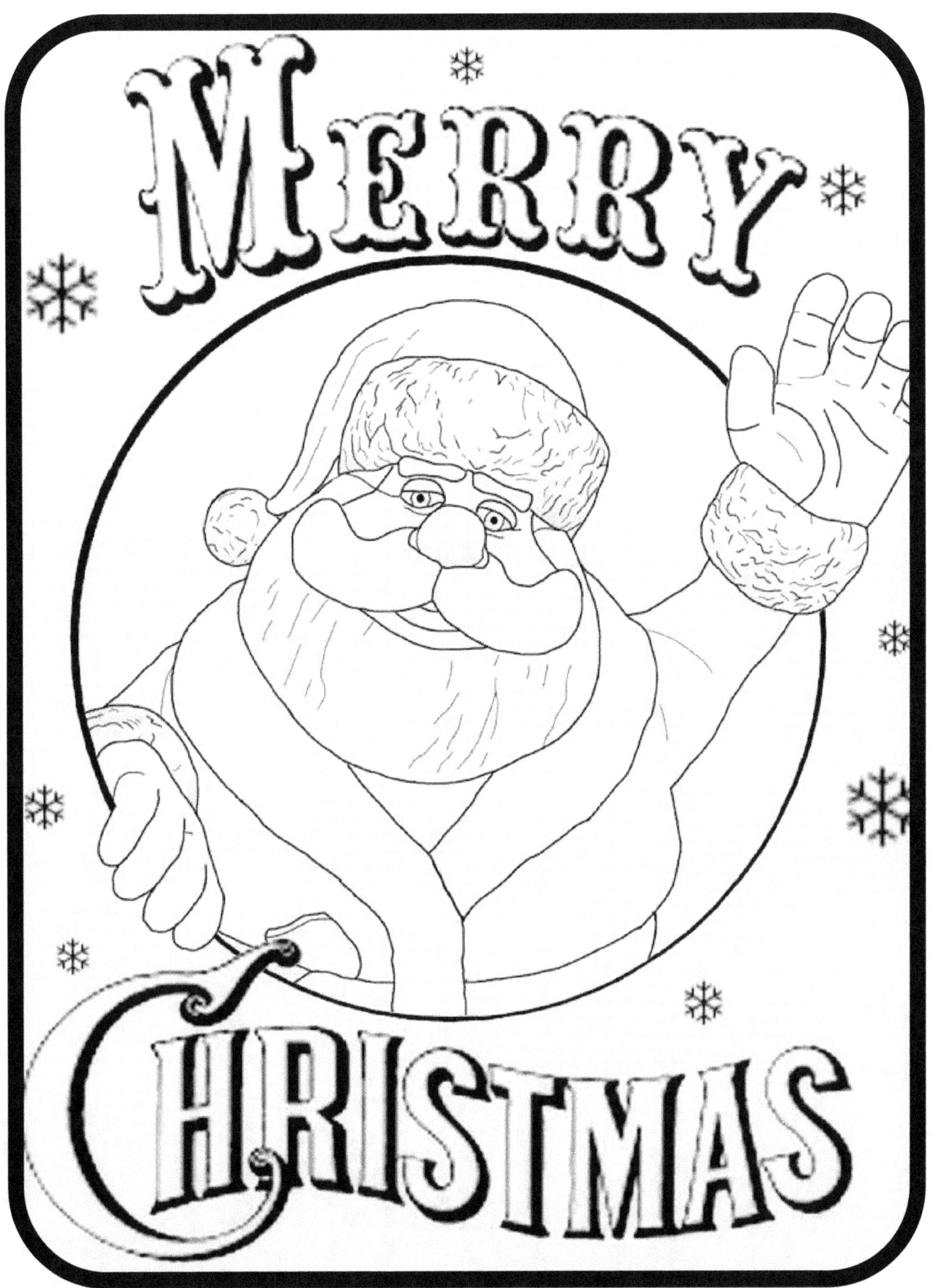

MERRY
CHRISTMAS

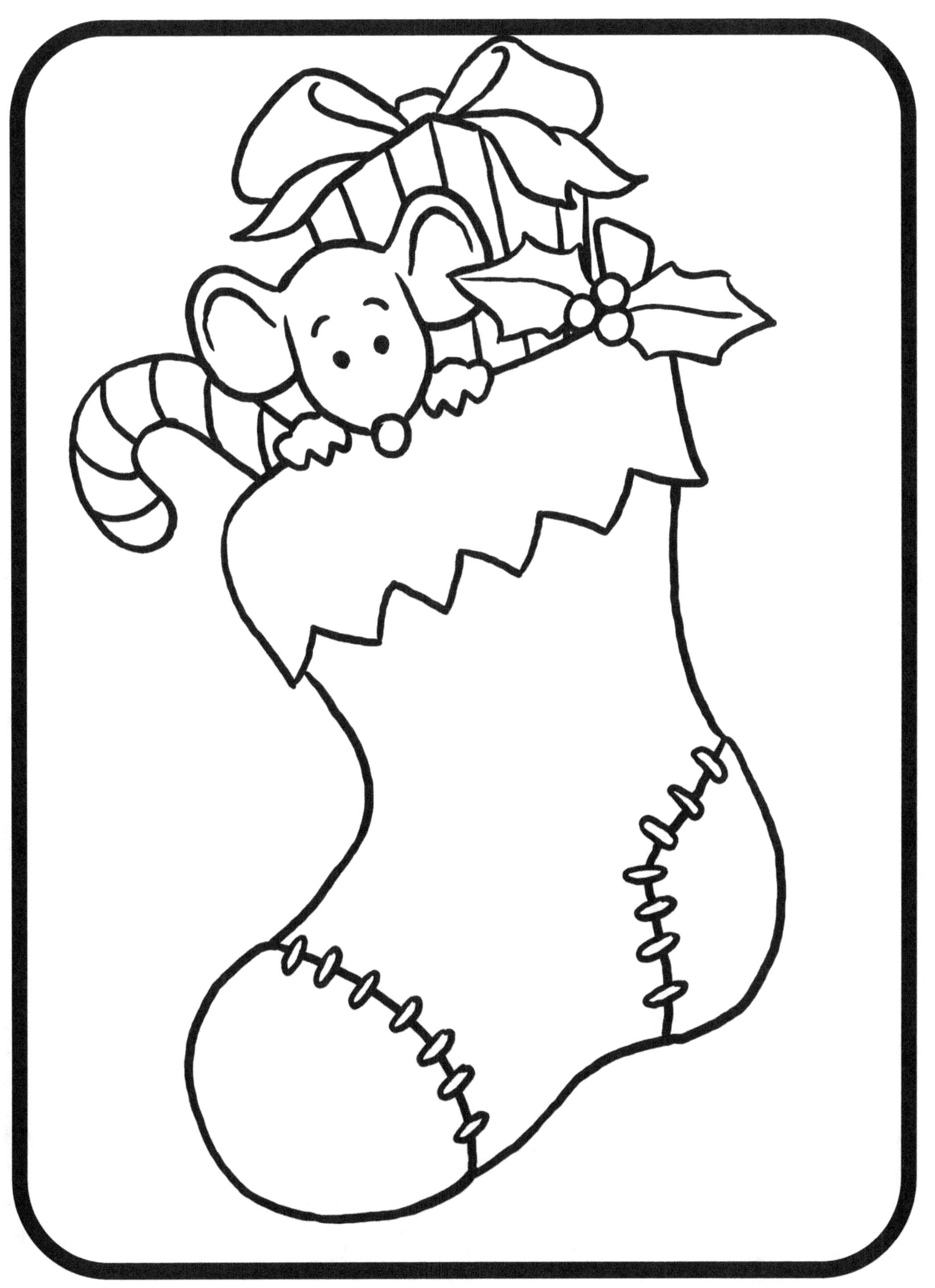

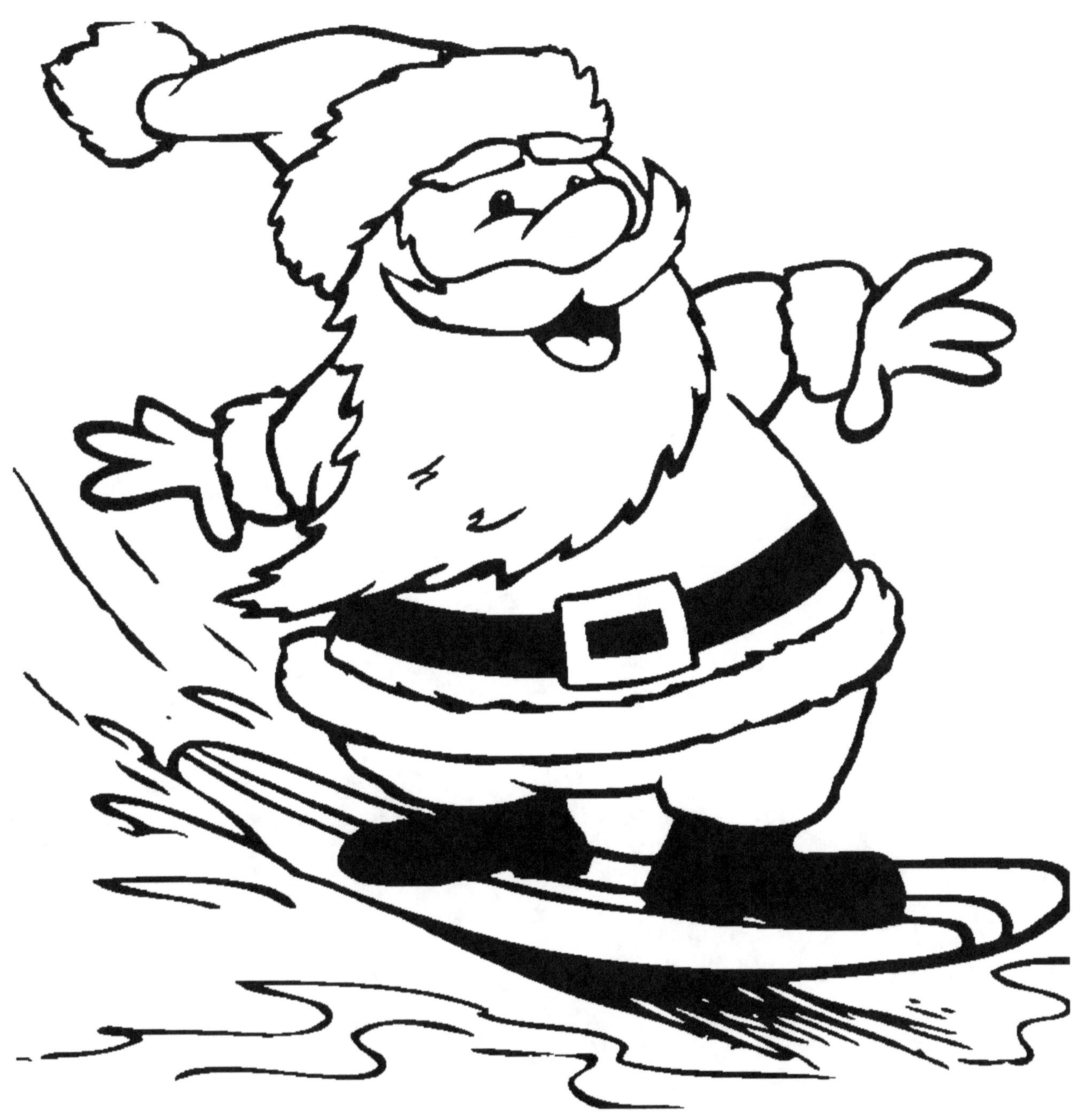

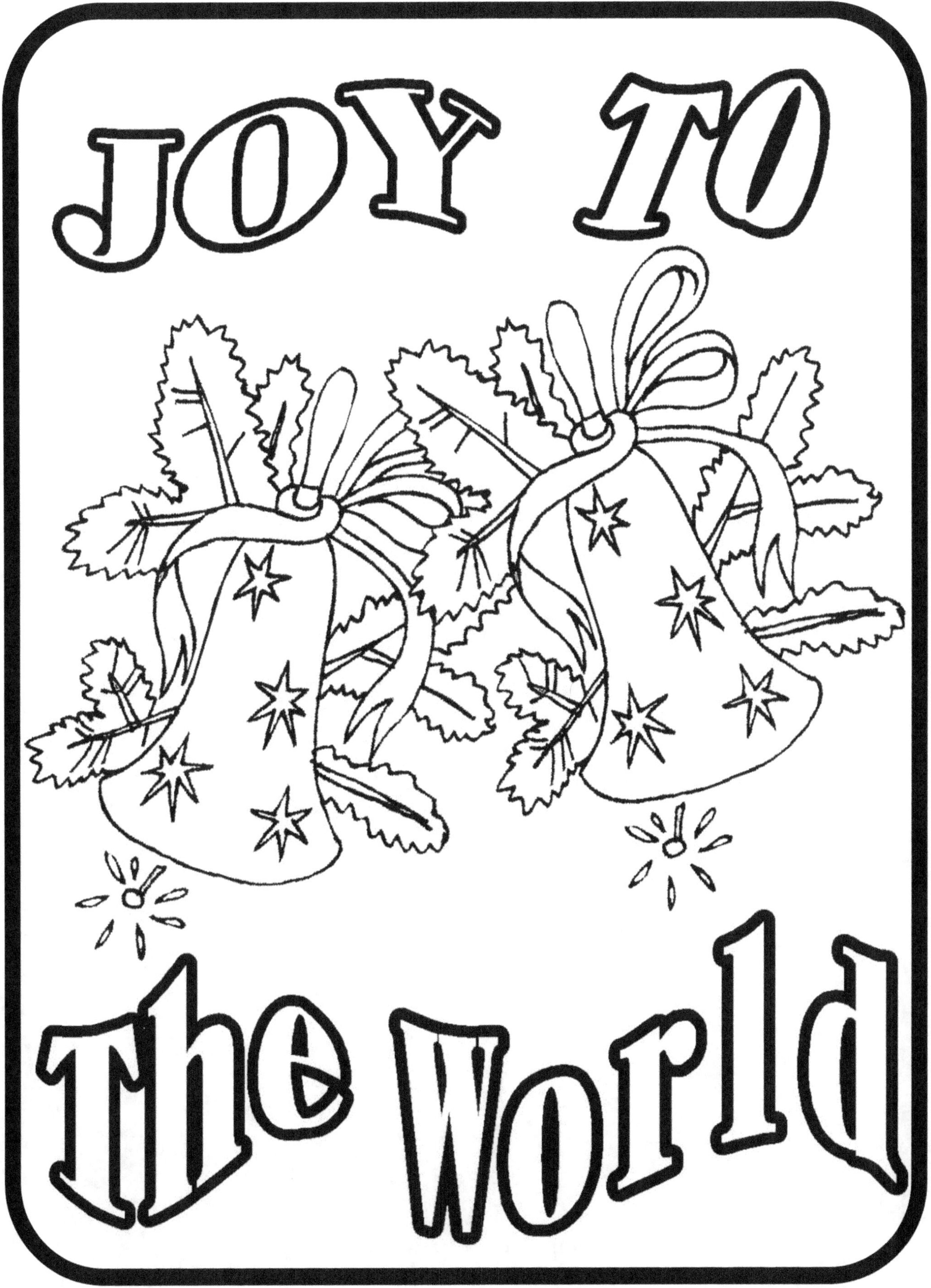

JOY TO
THE World

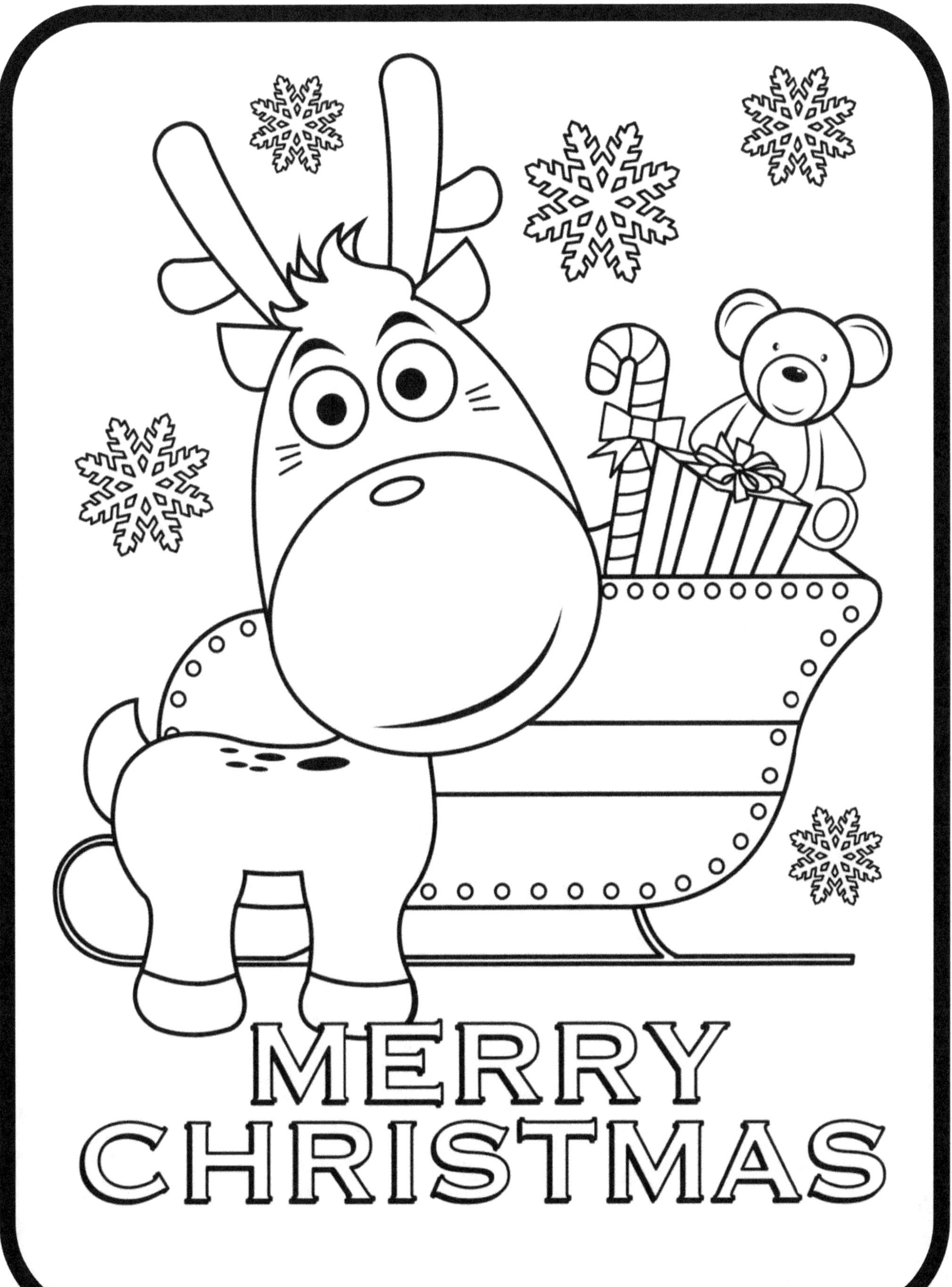

MERRY
CHRISTMAS

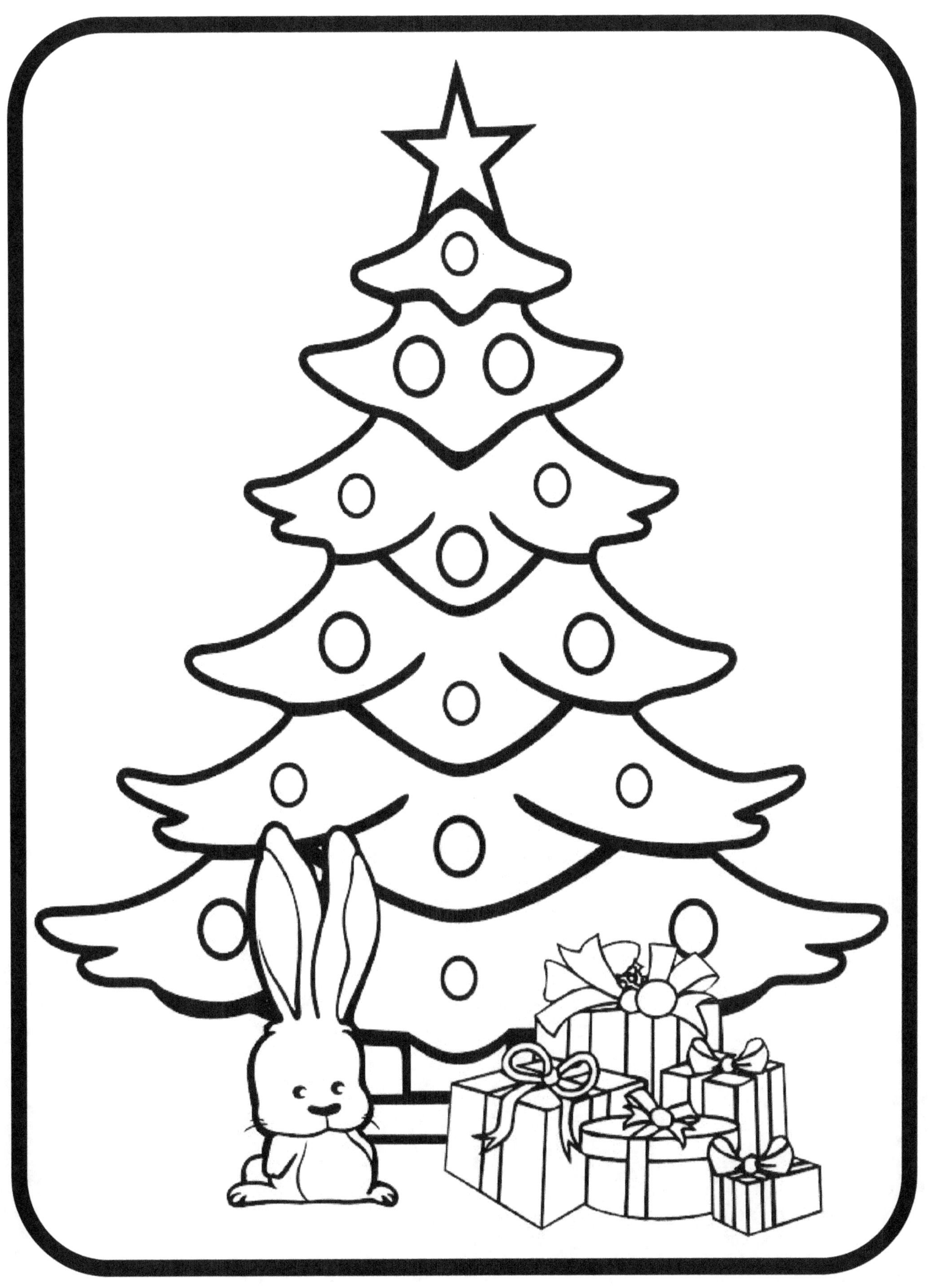

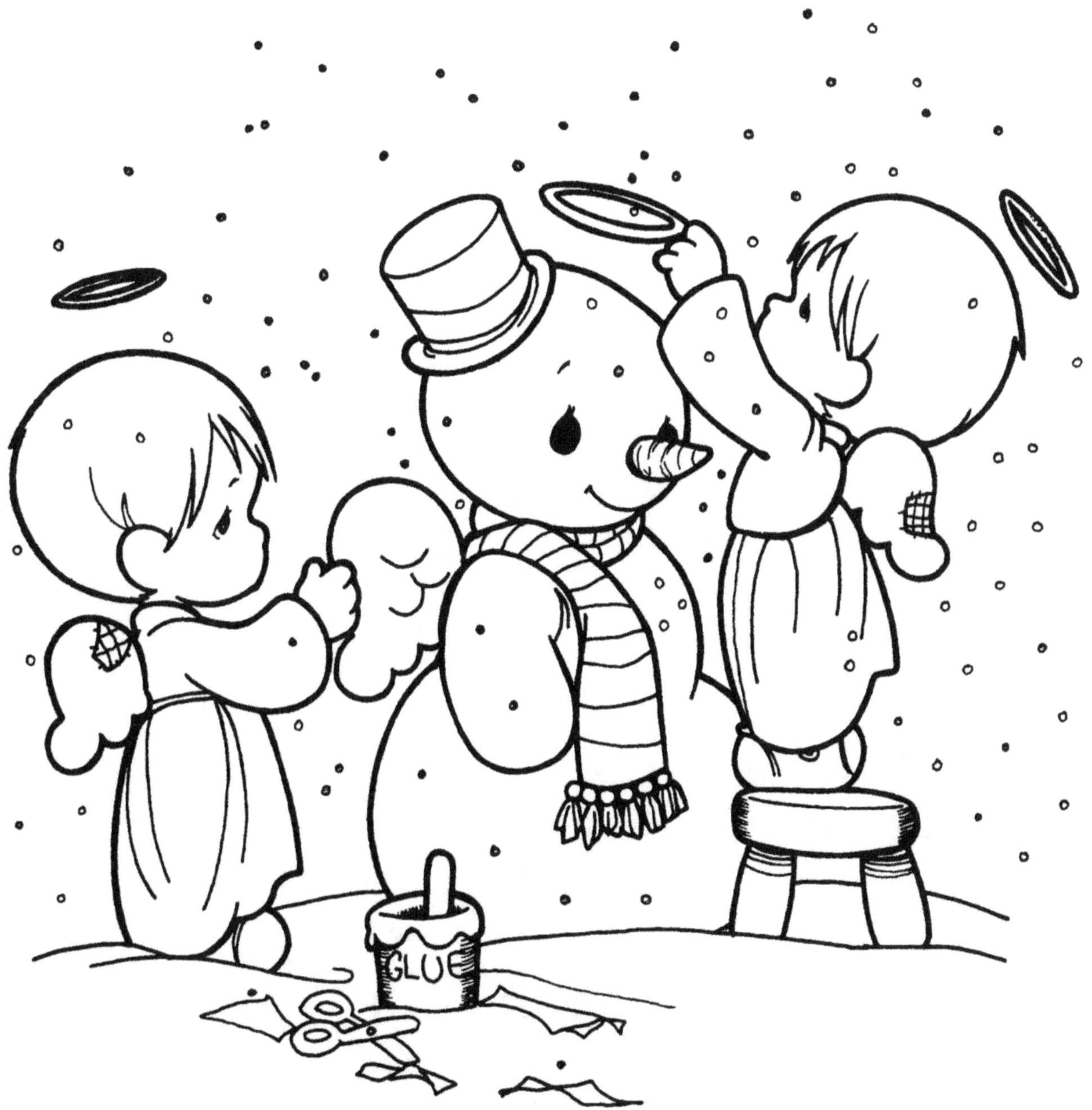

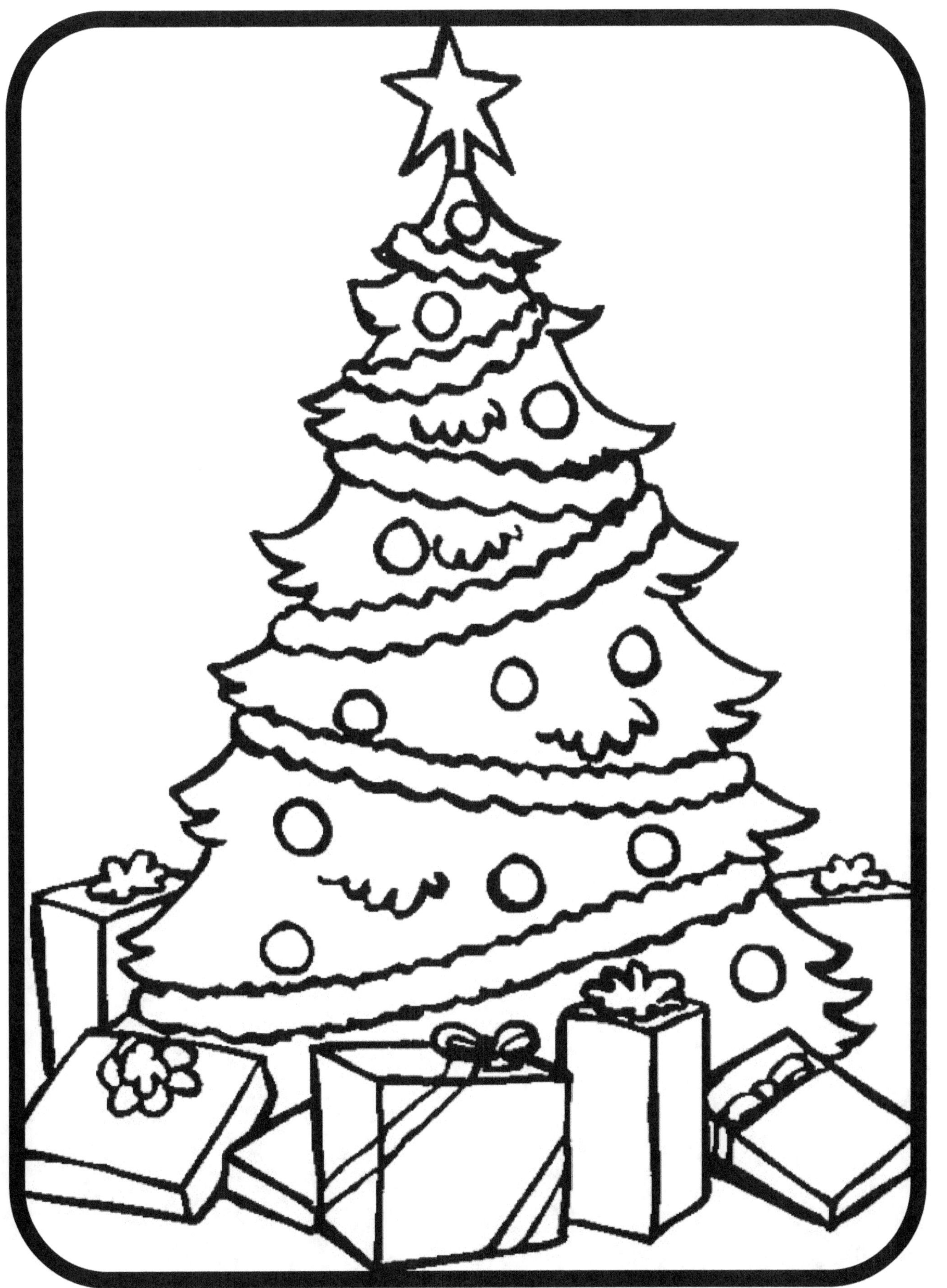

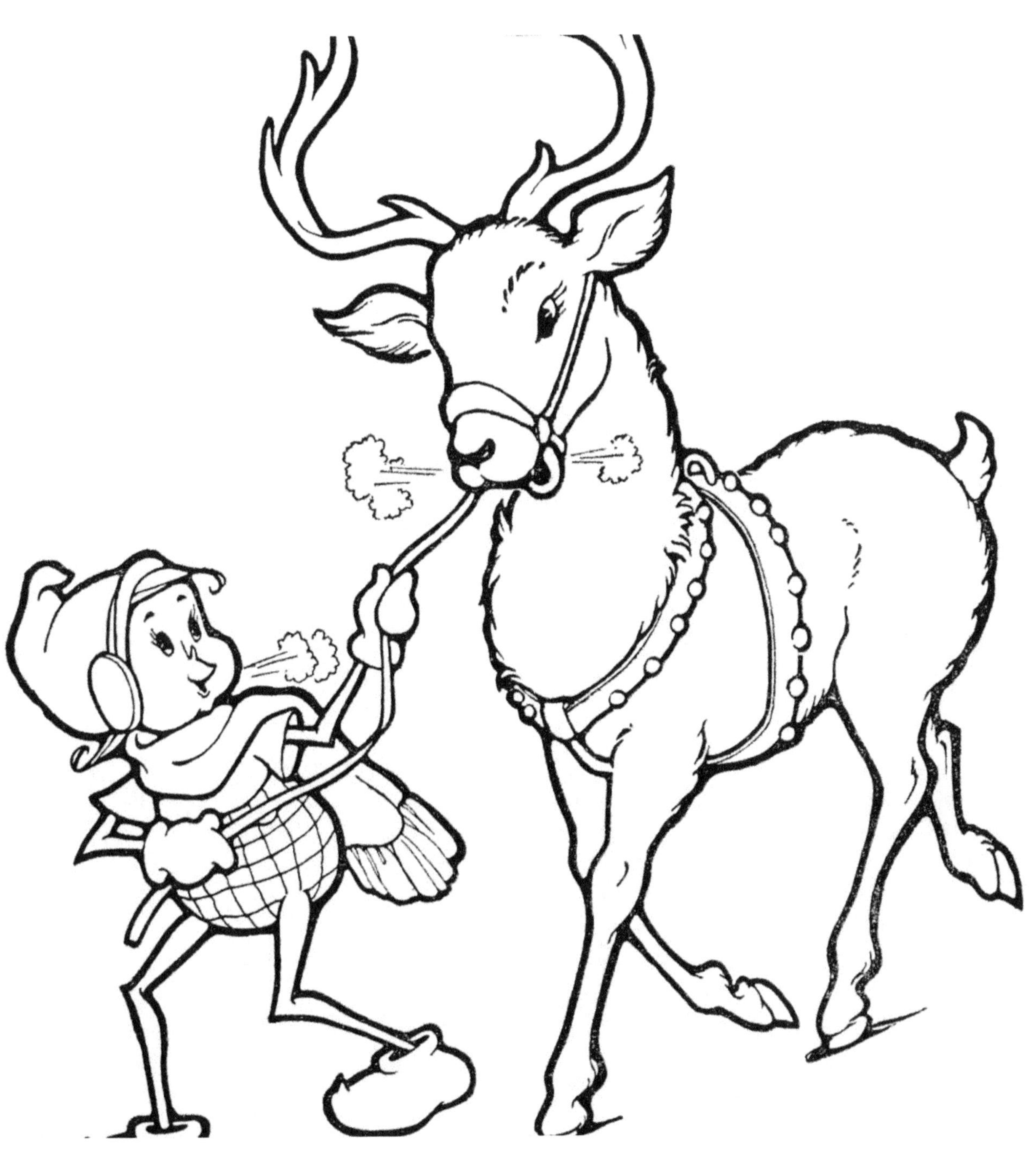

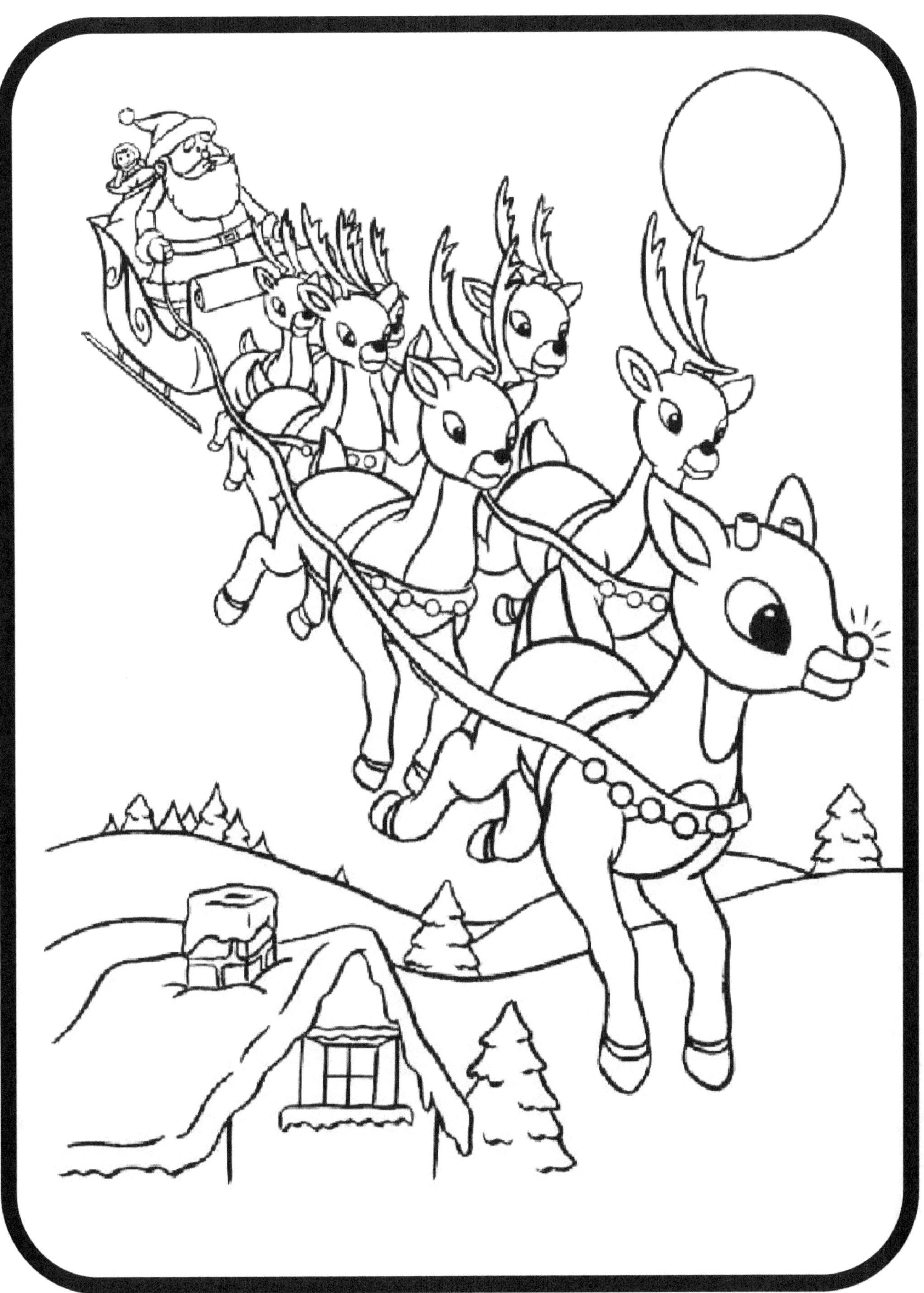

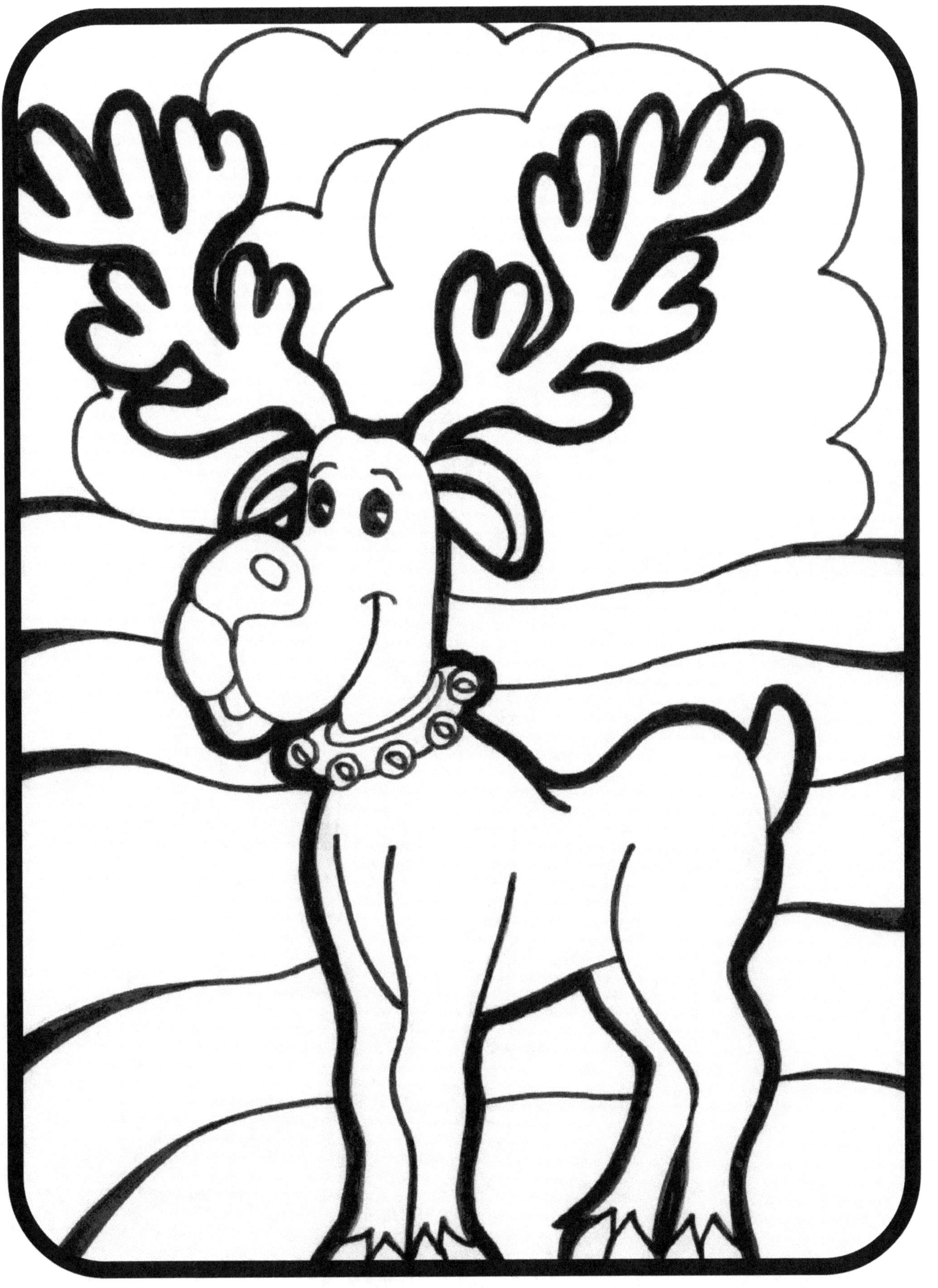

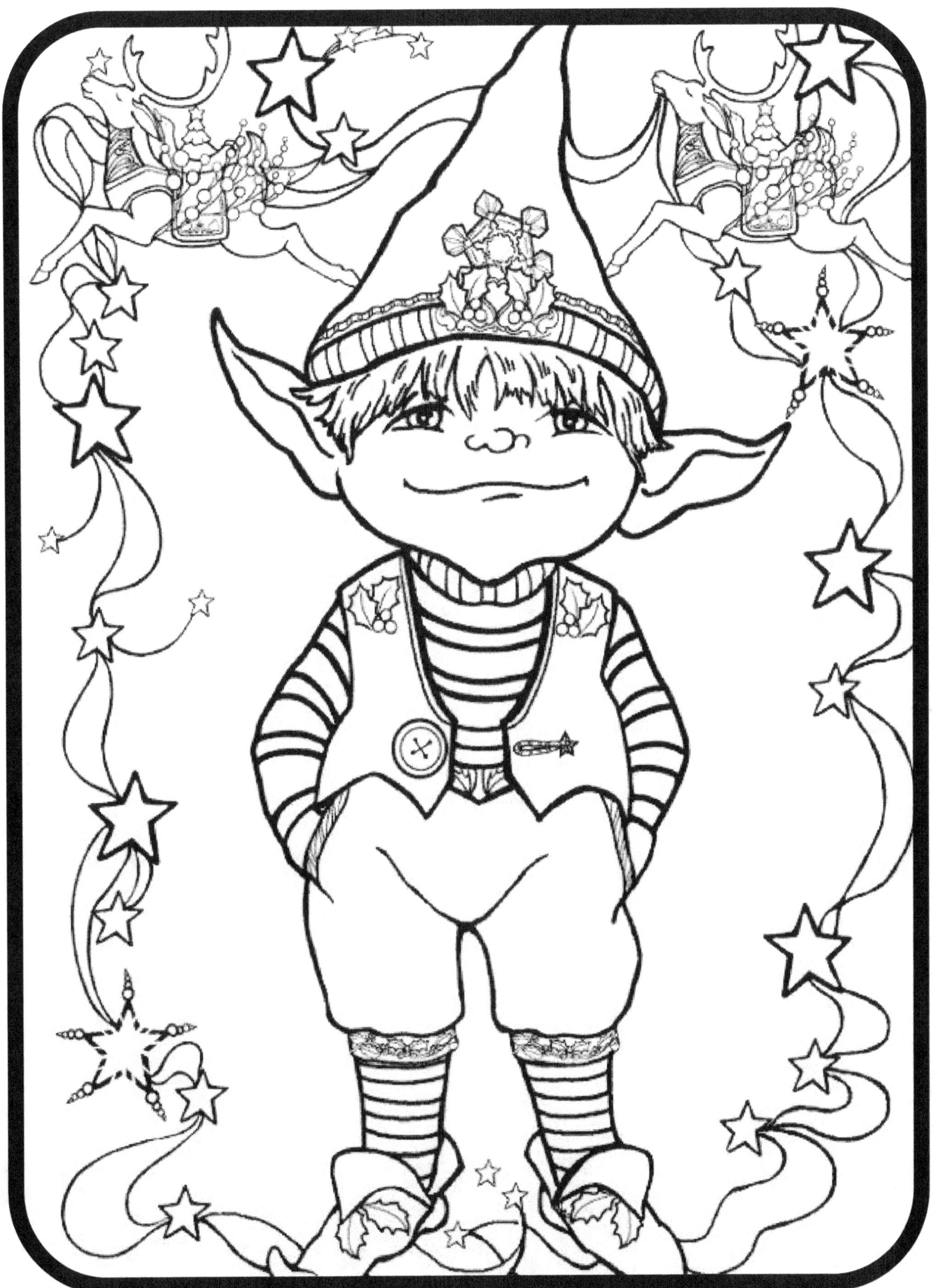

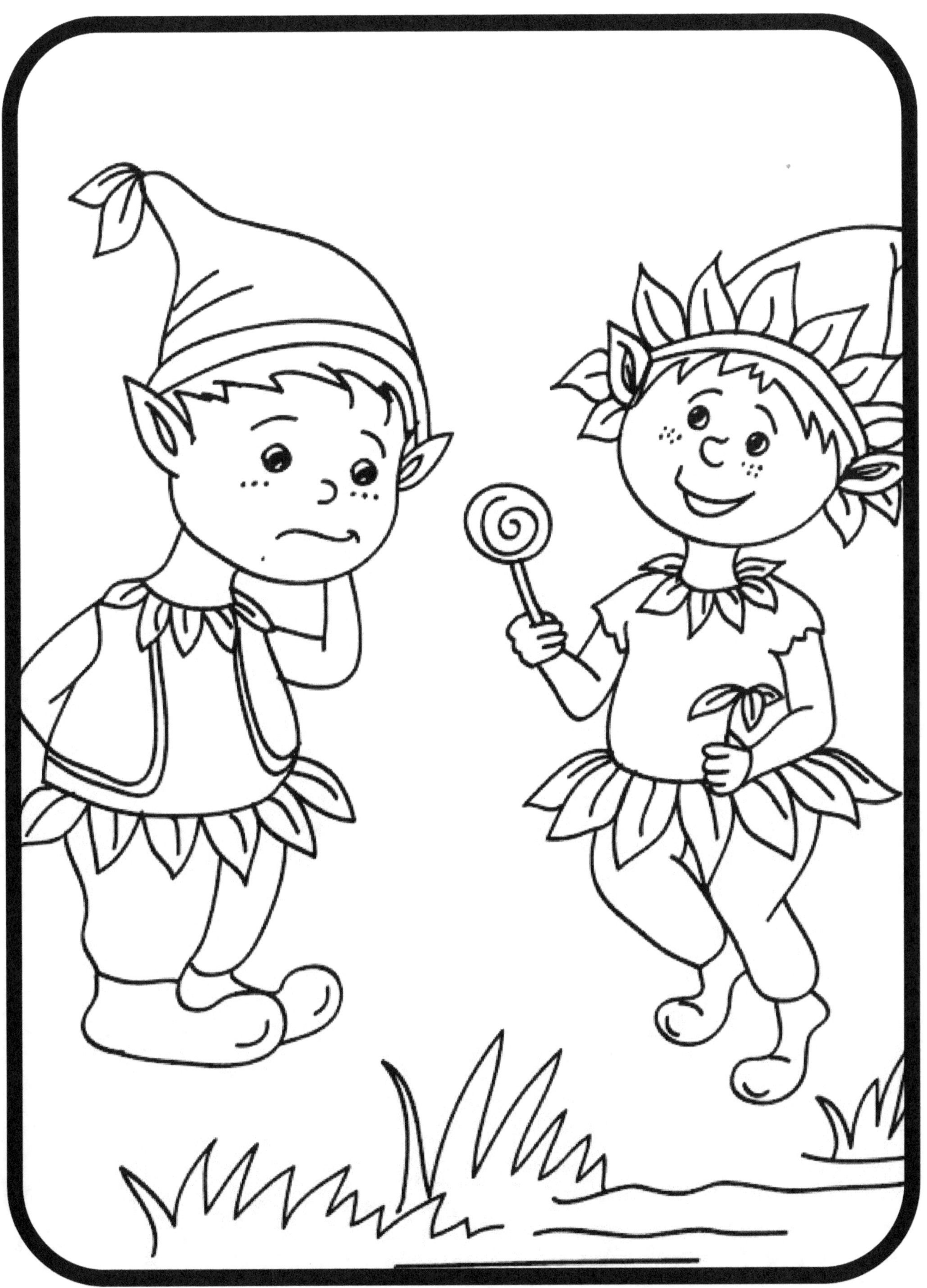

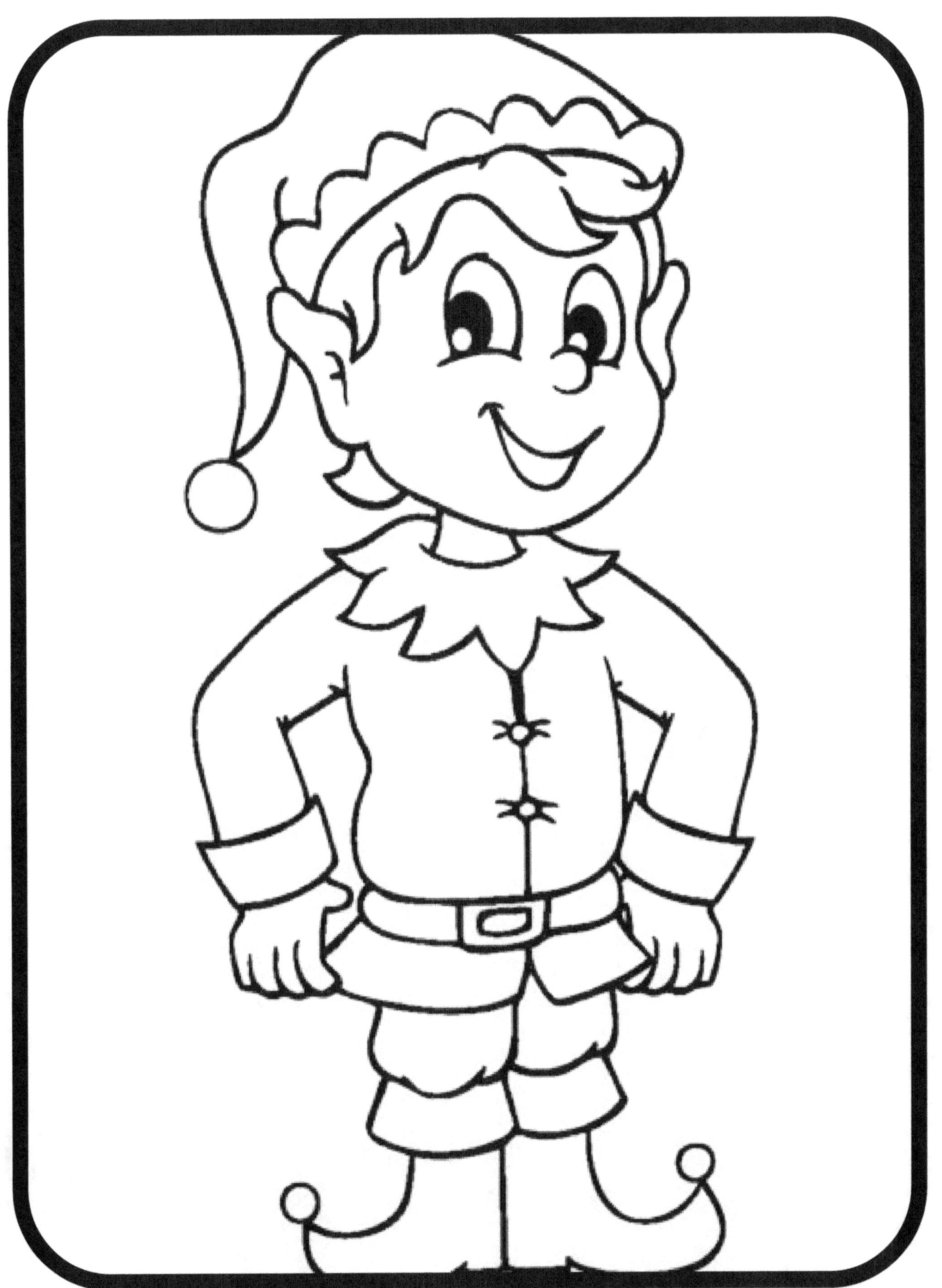

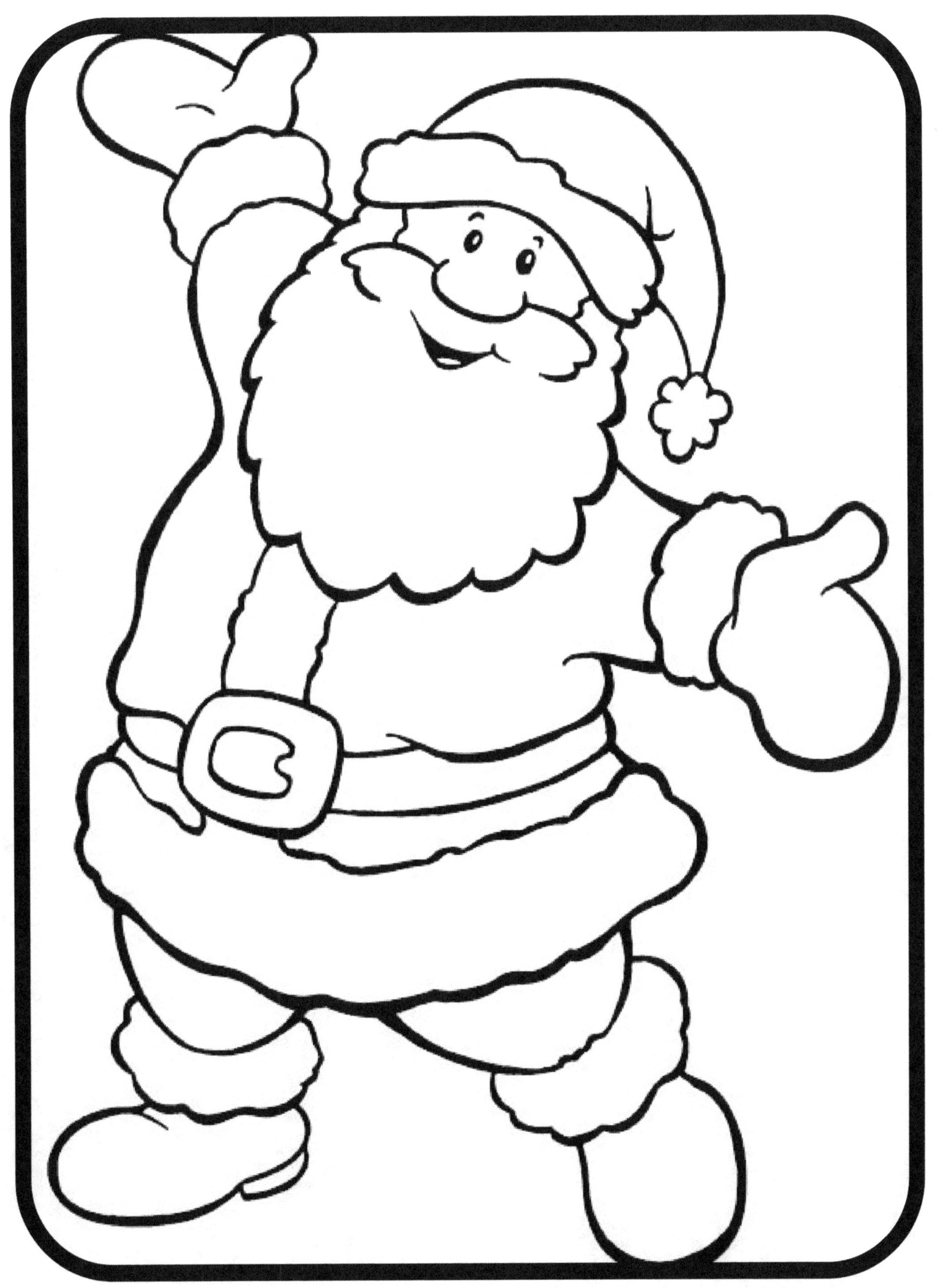

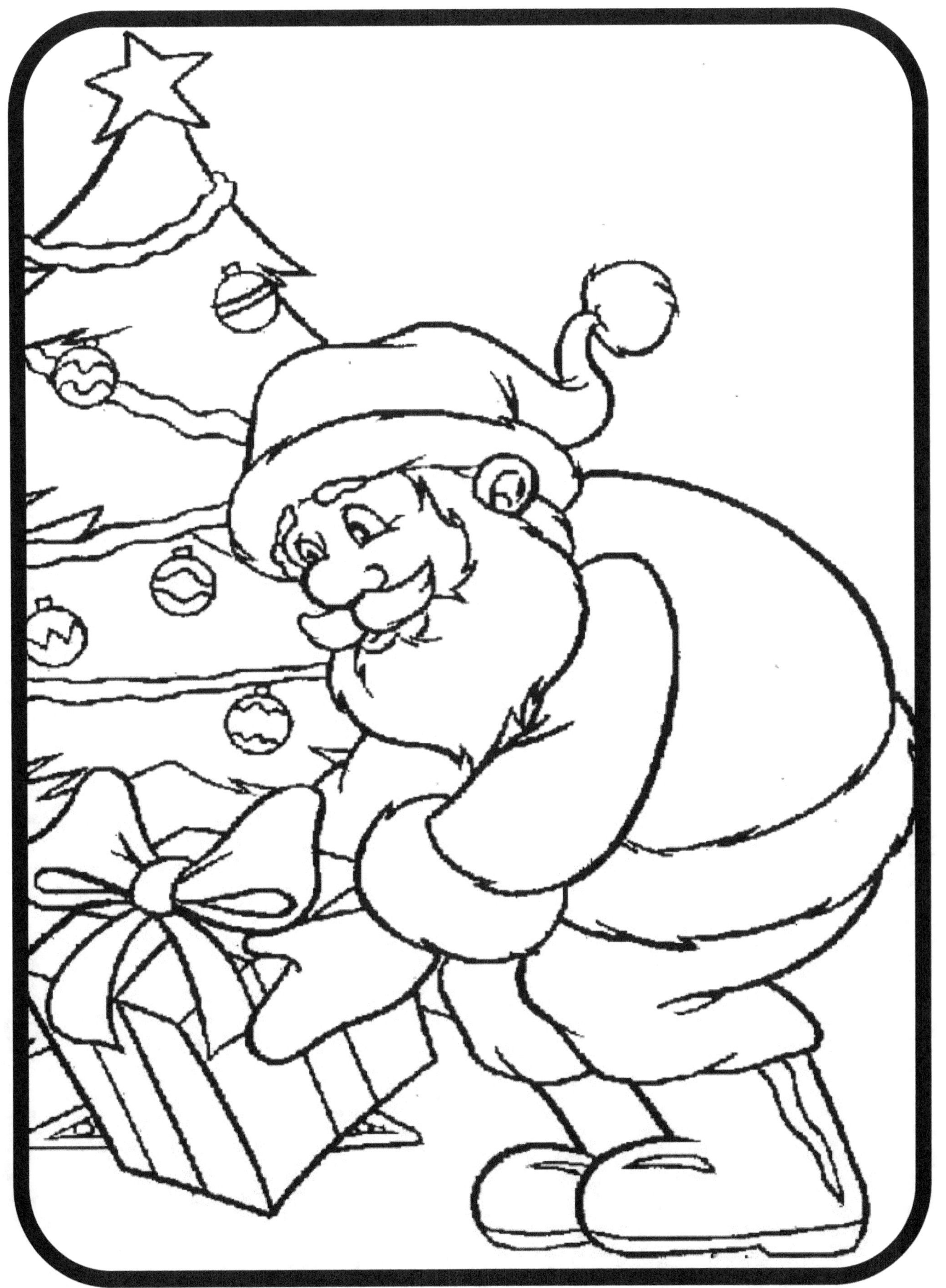

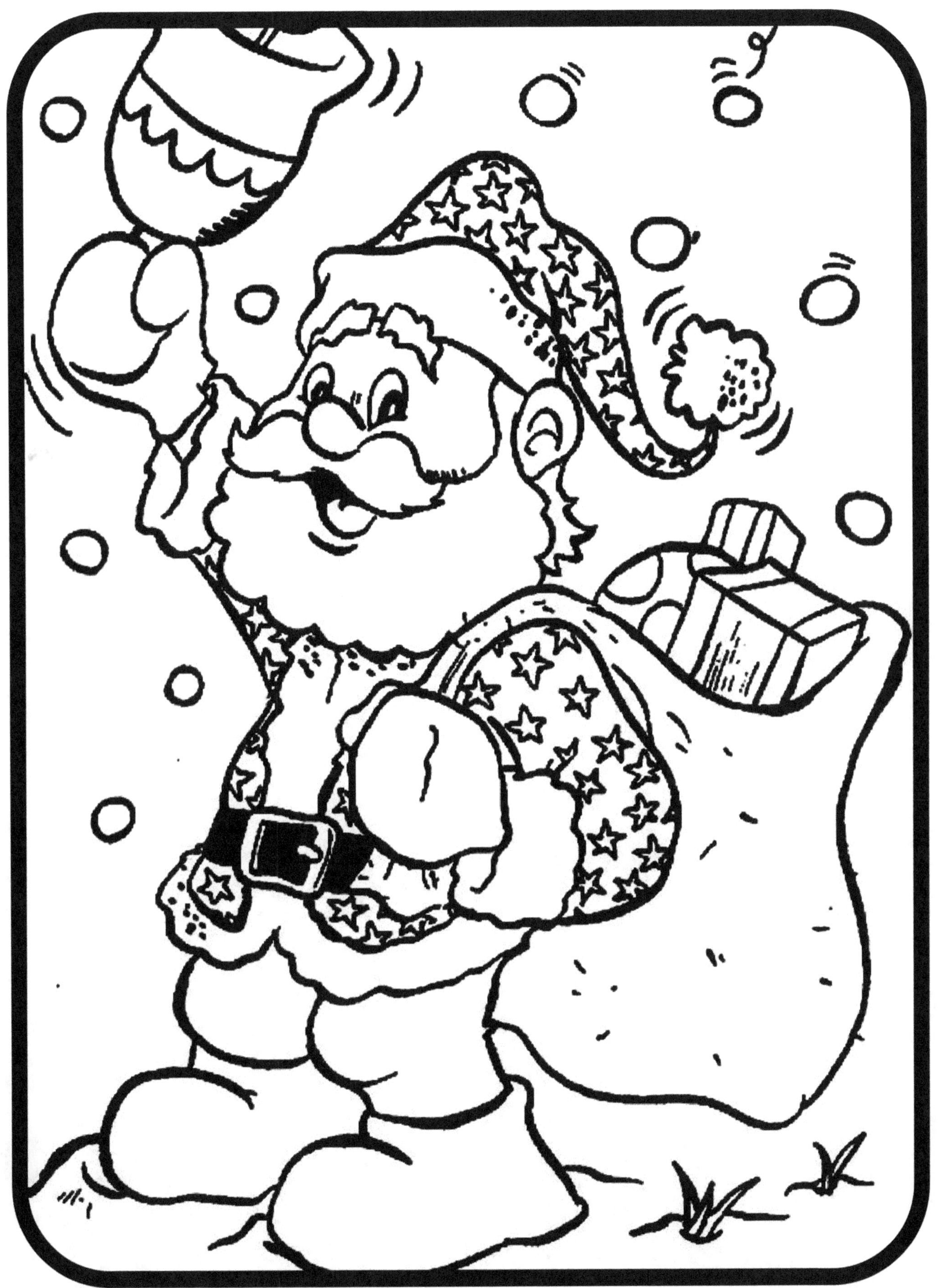

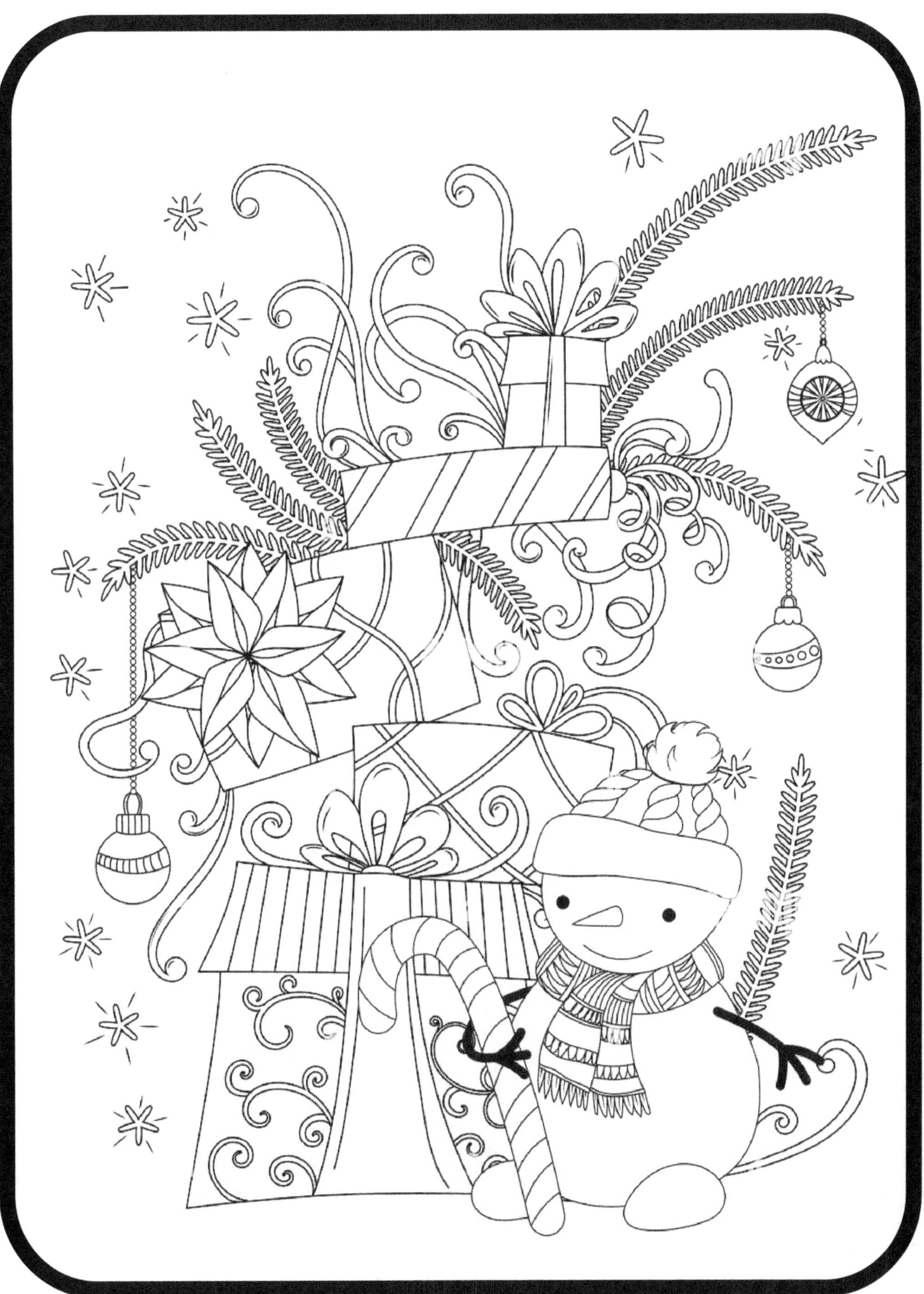

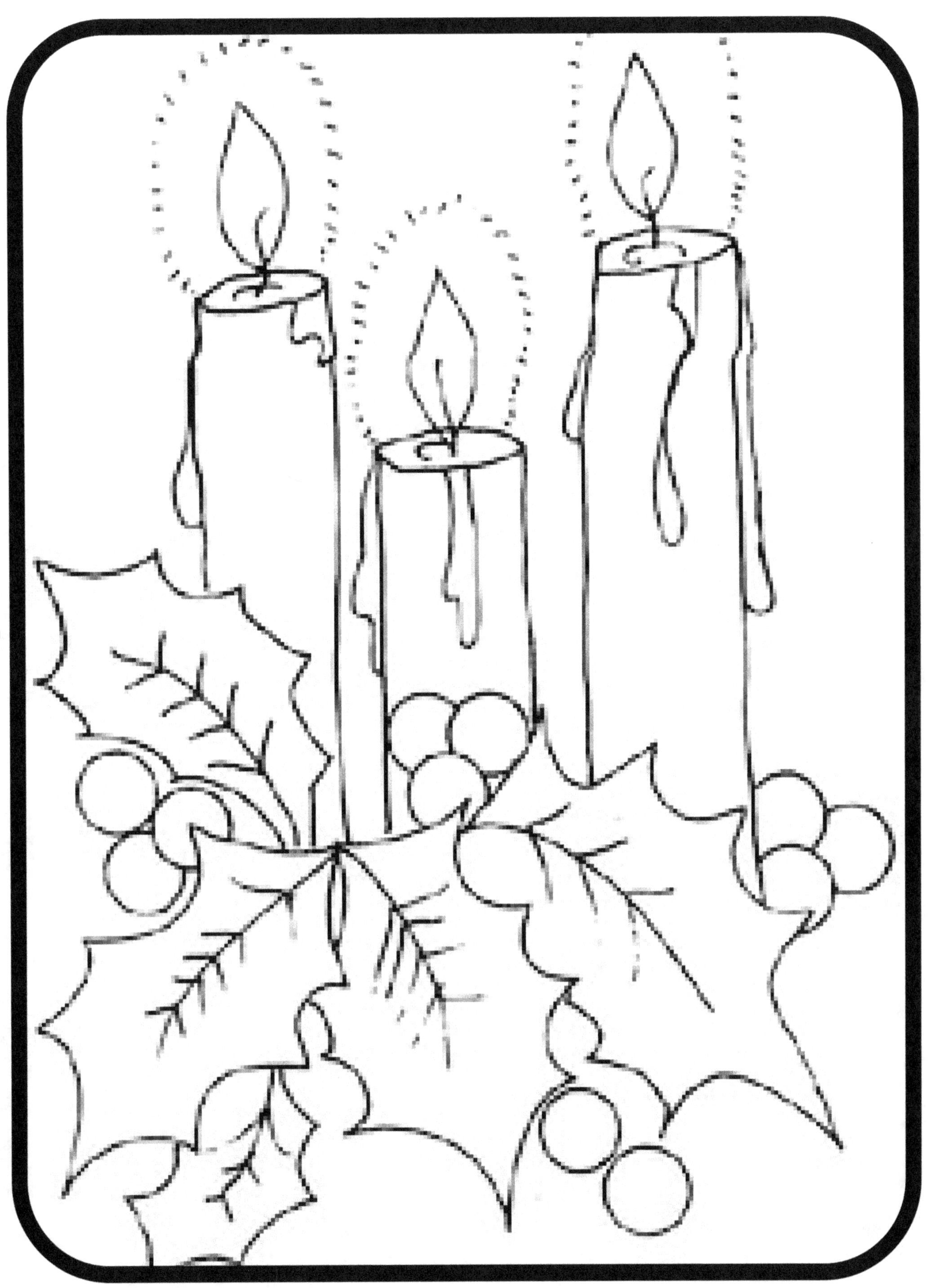

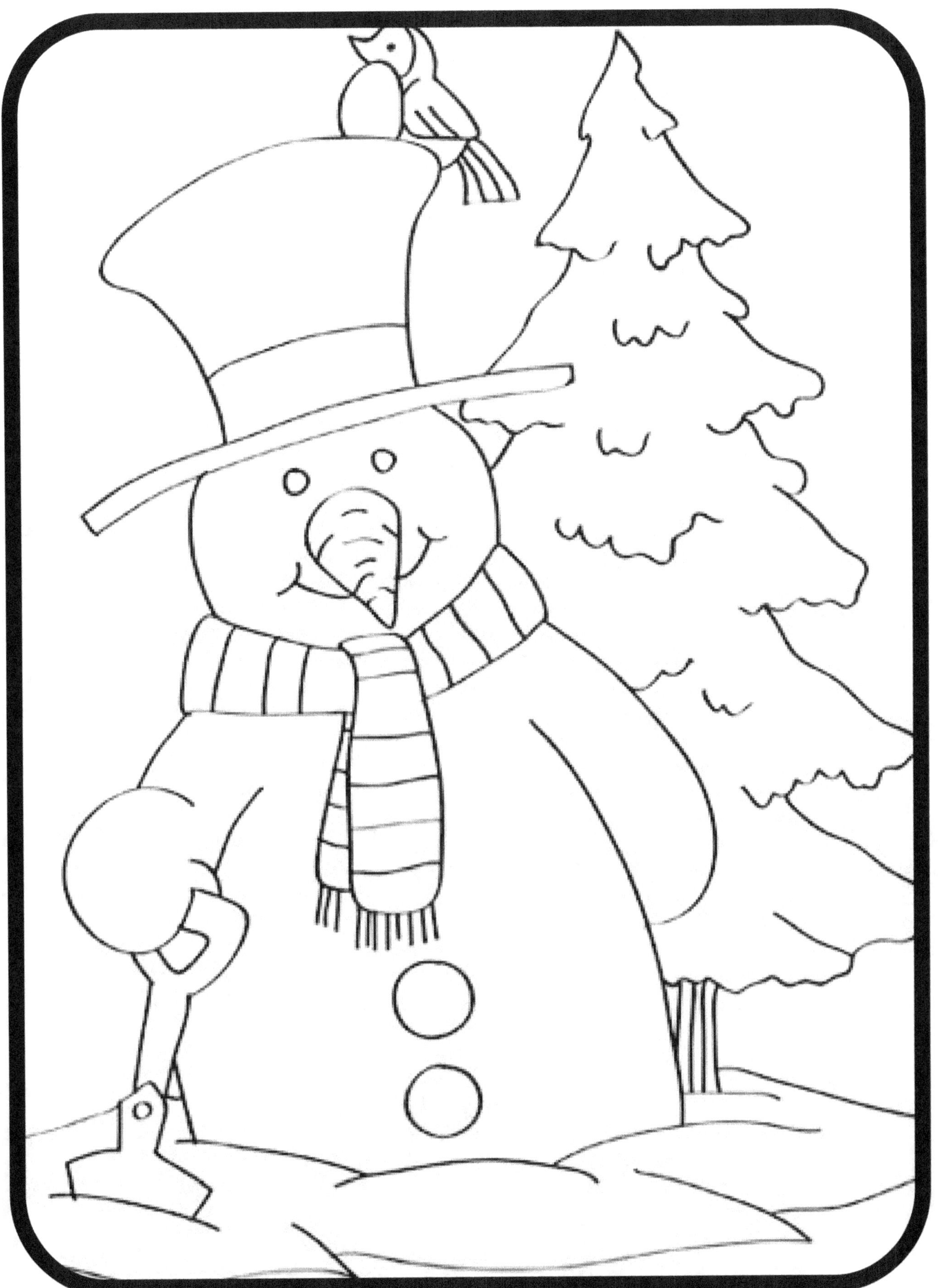

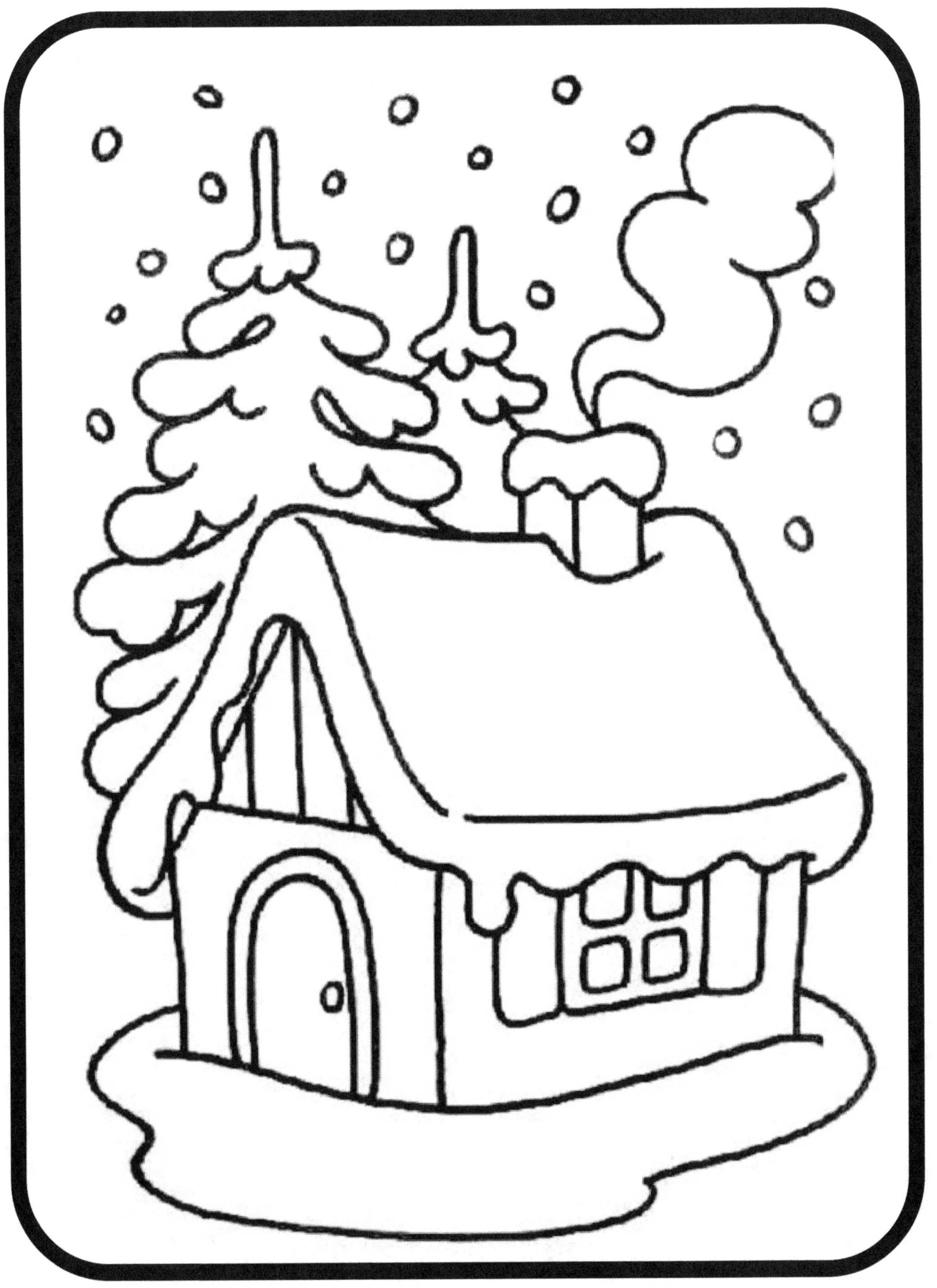

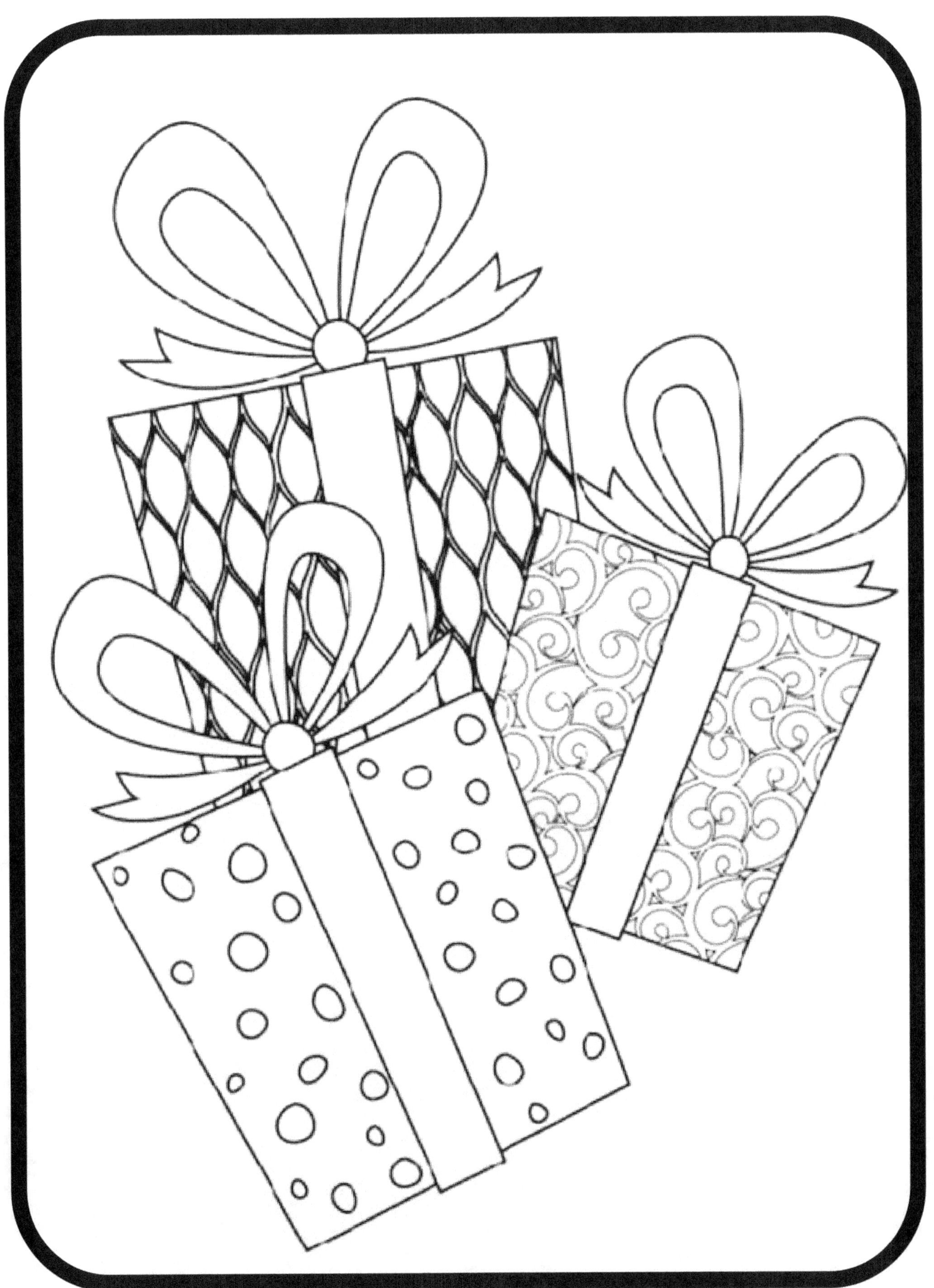

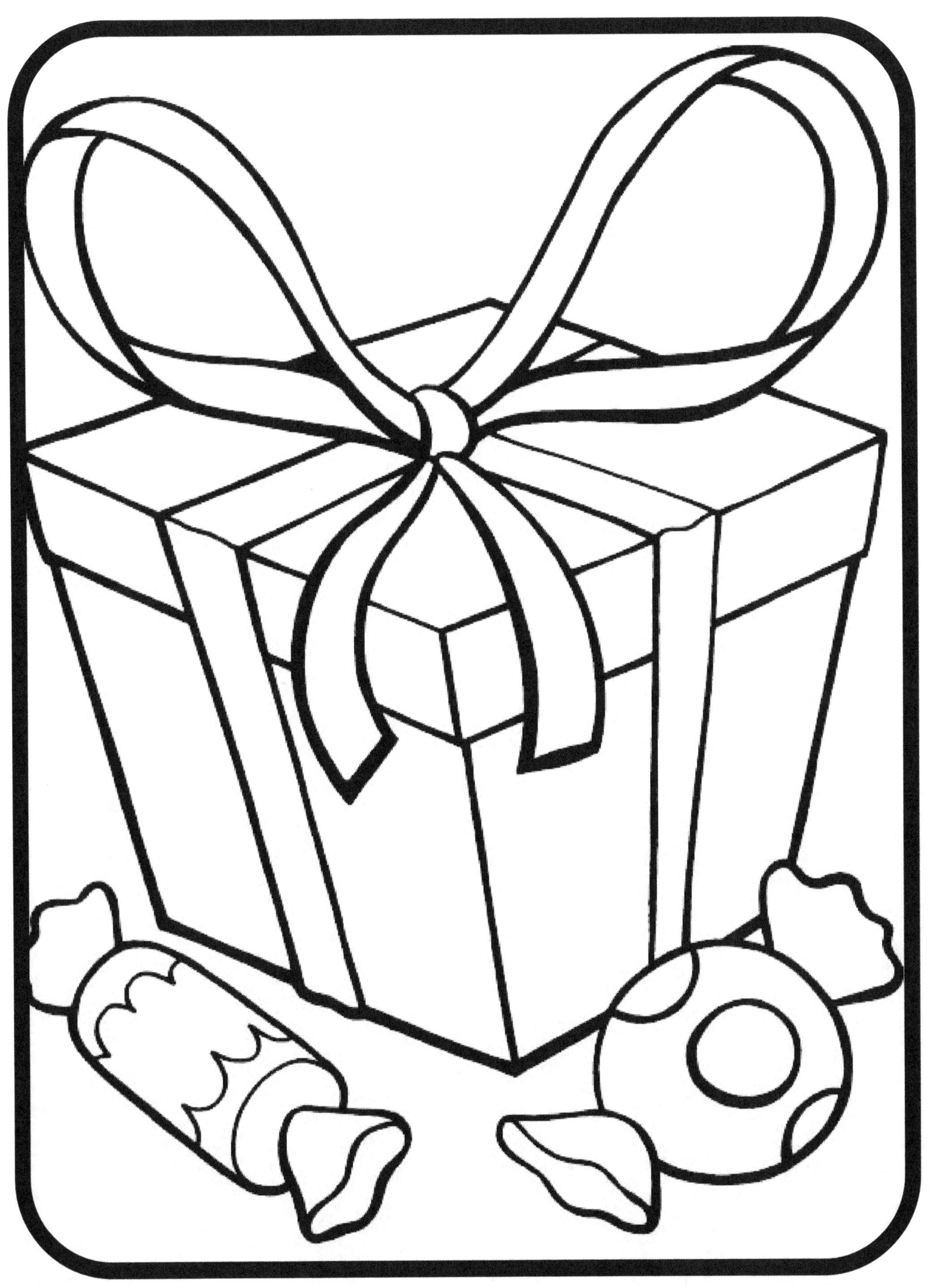

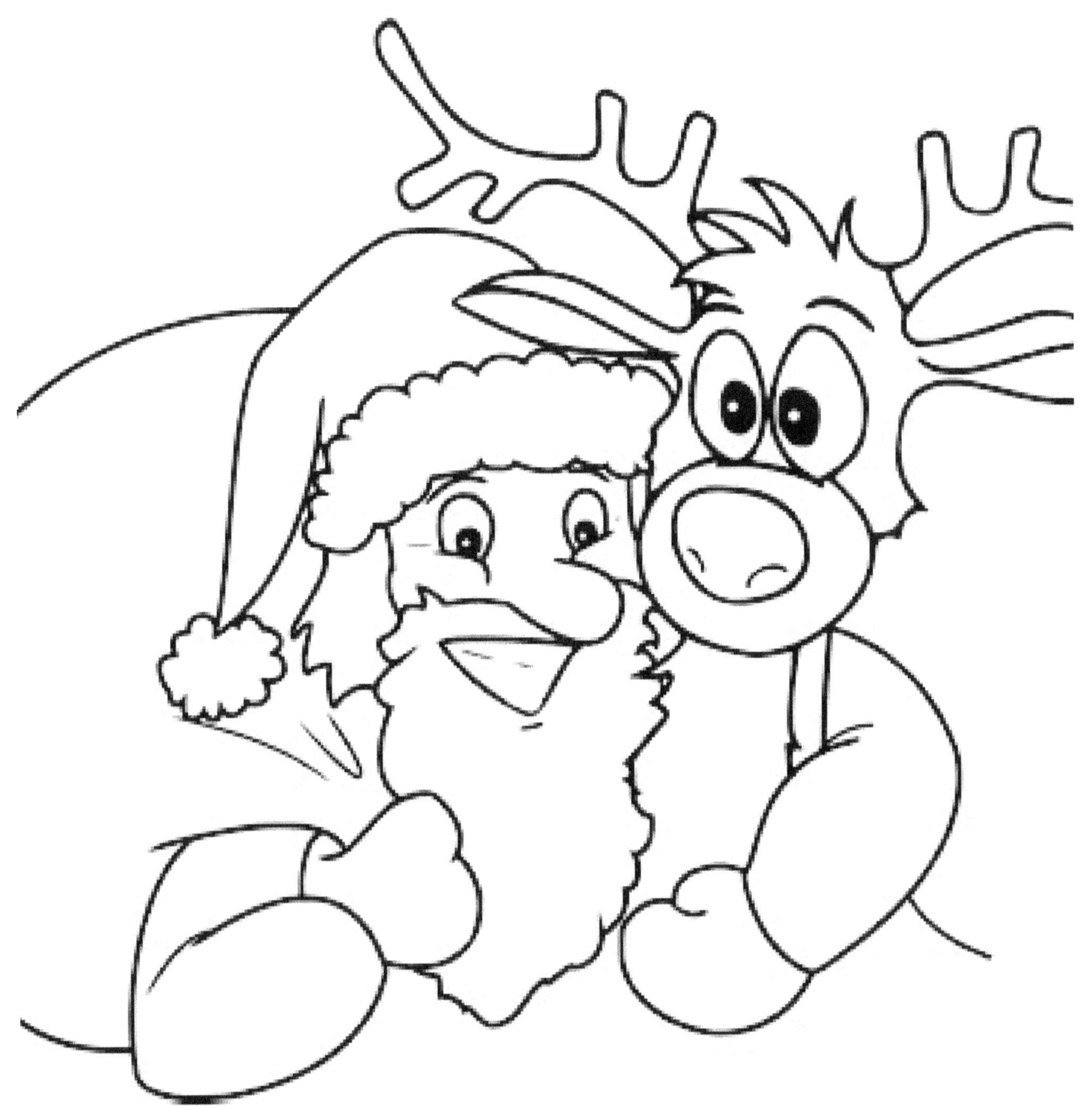

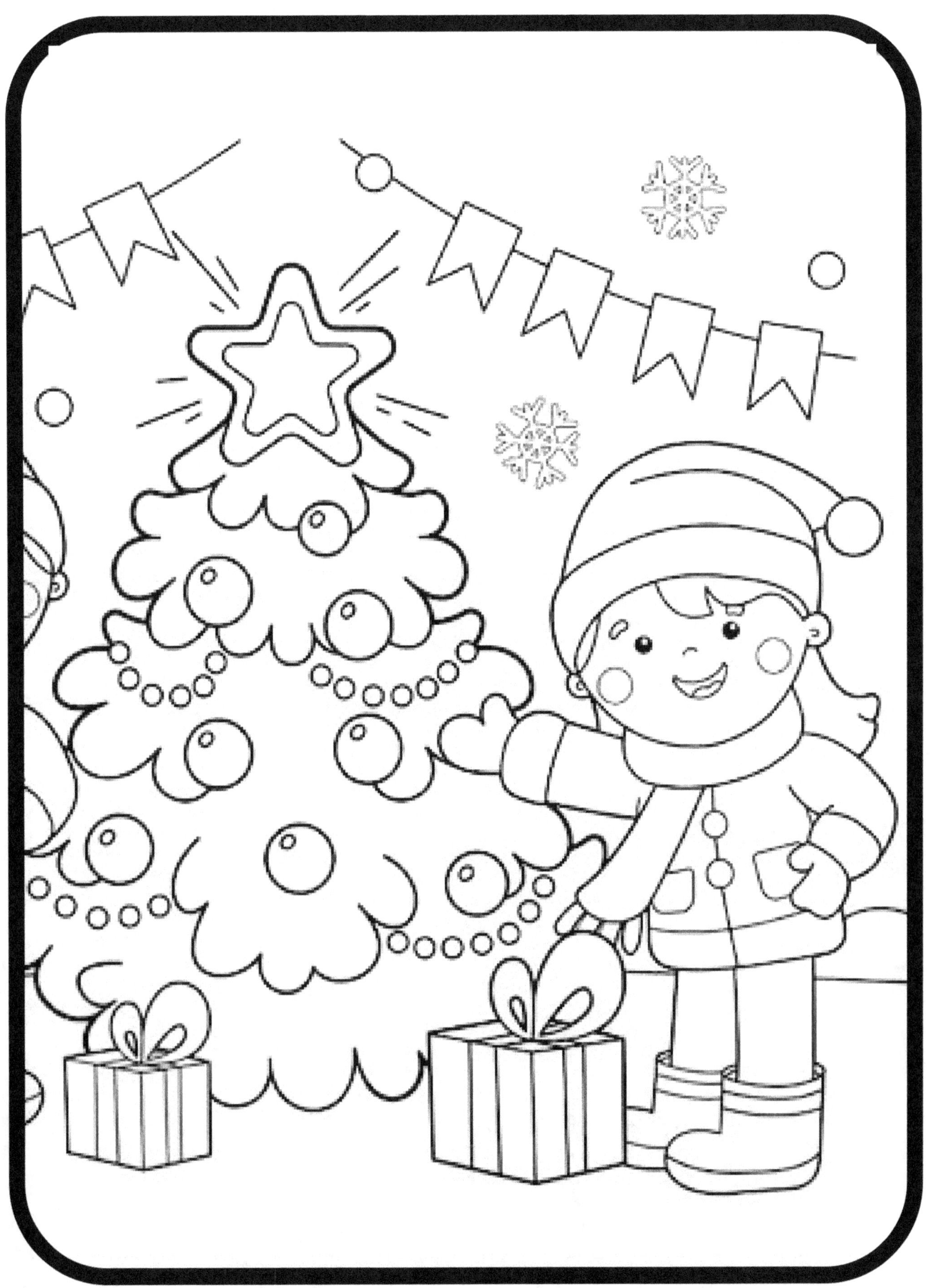

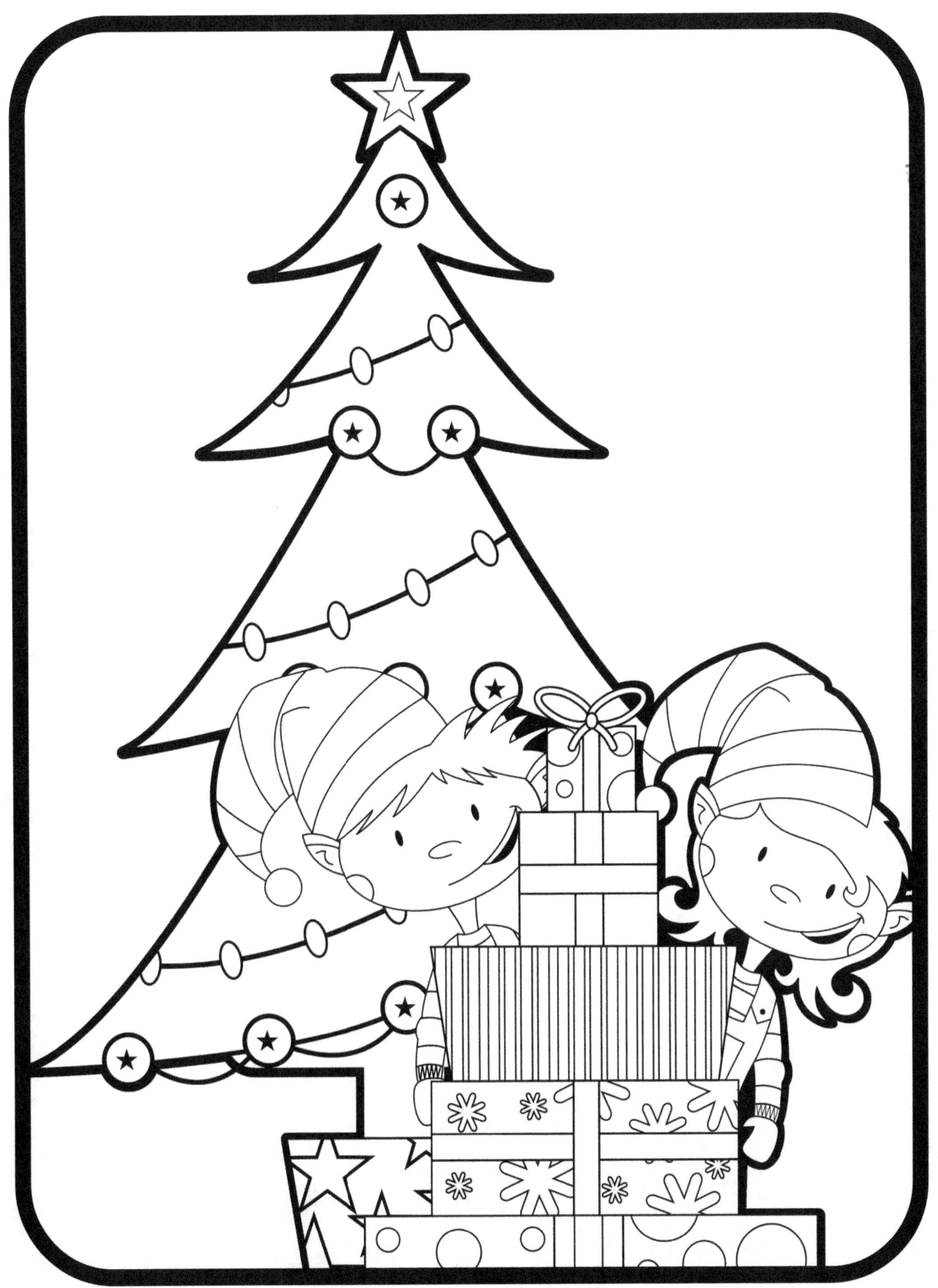

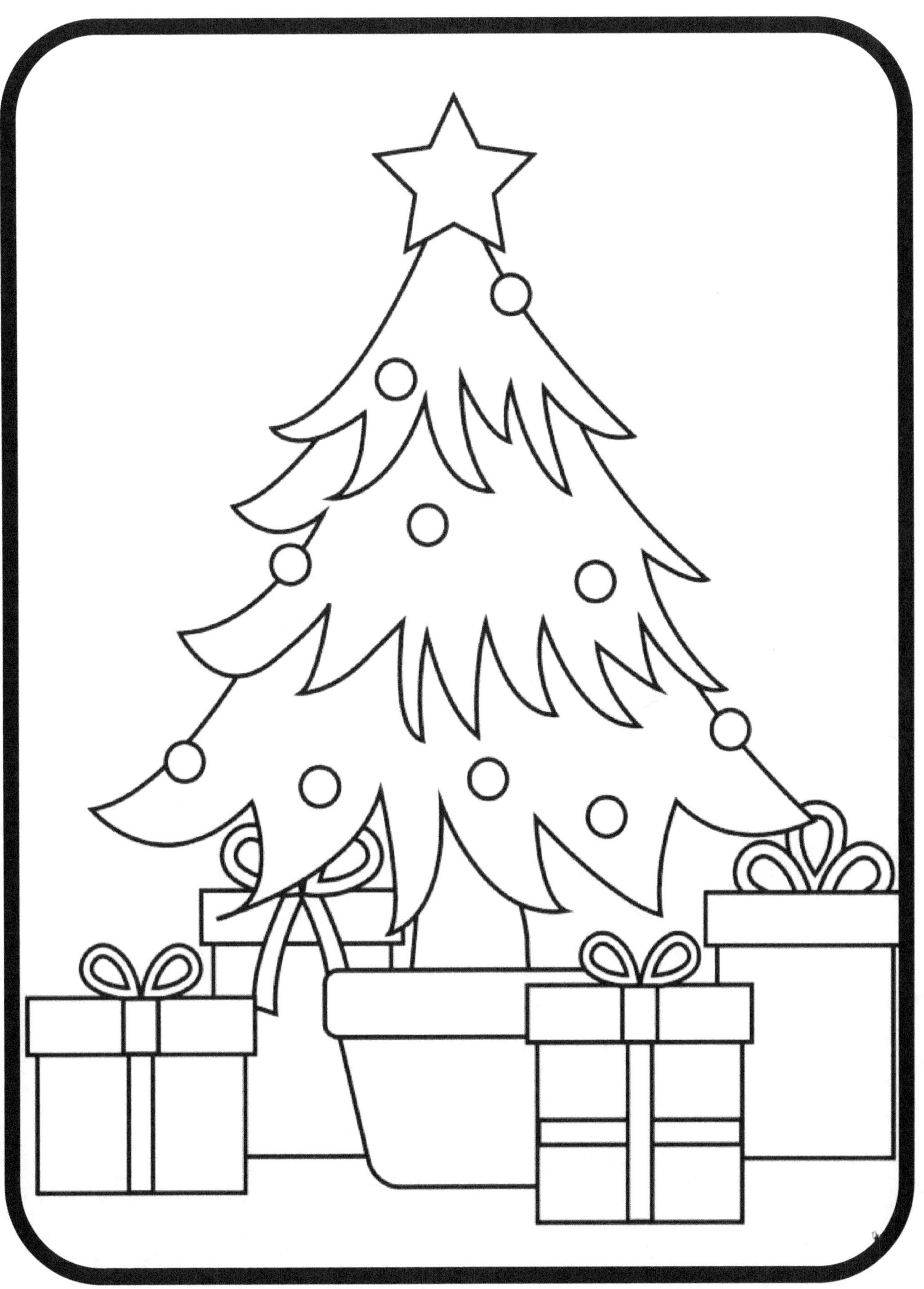

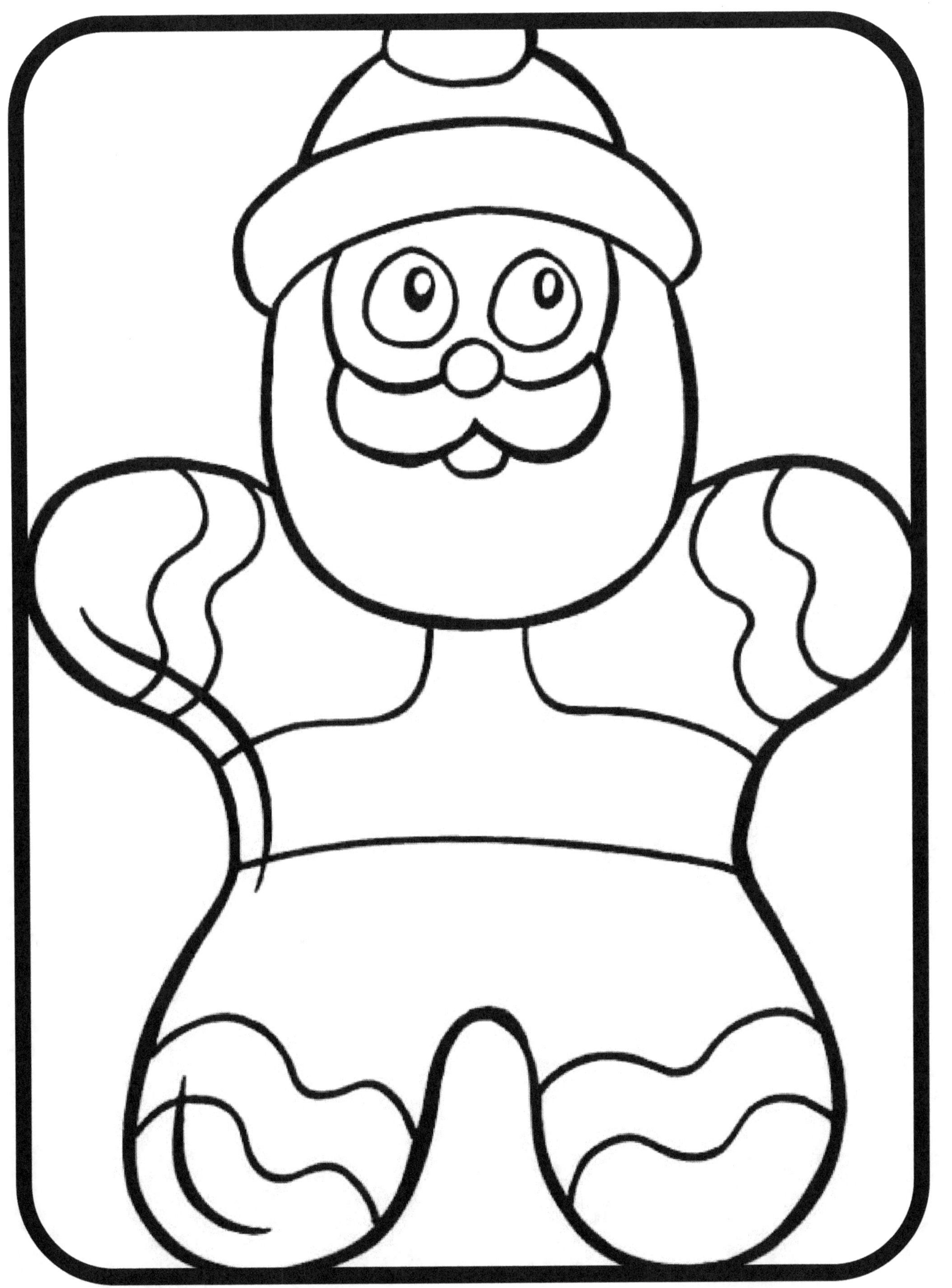

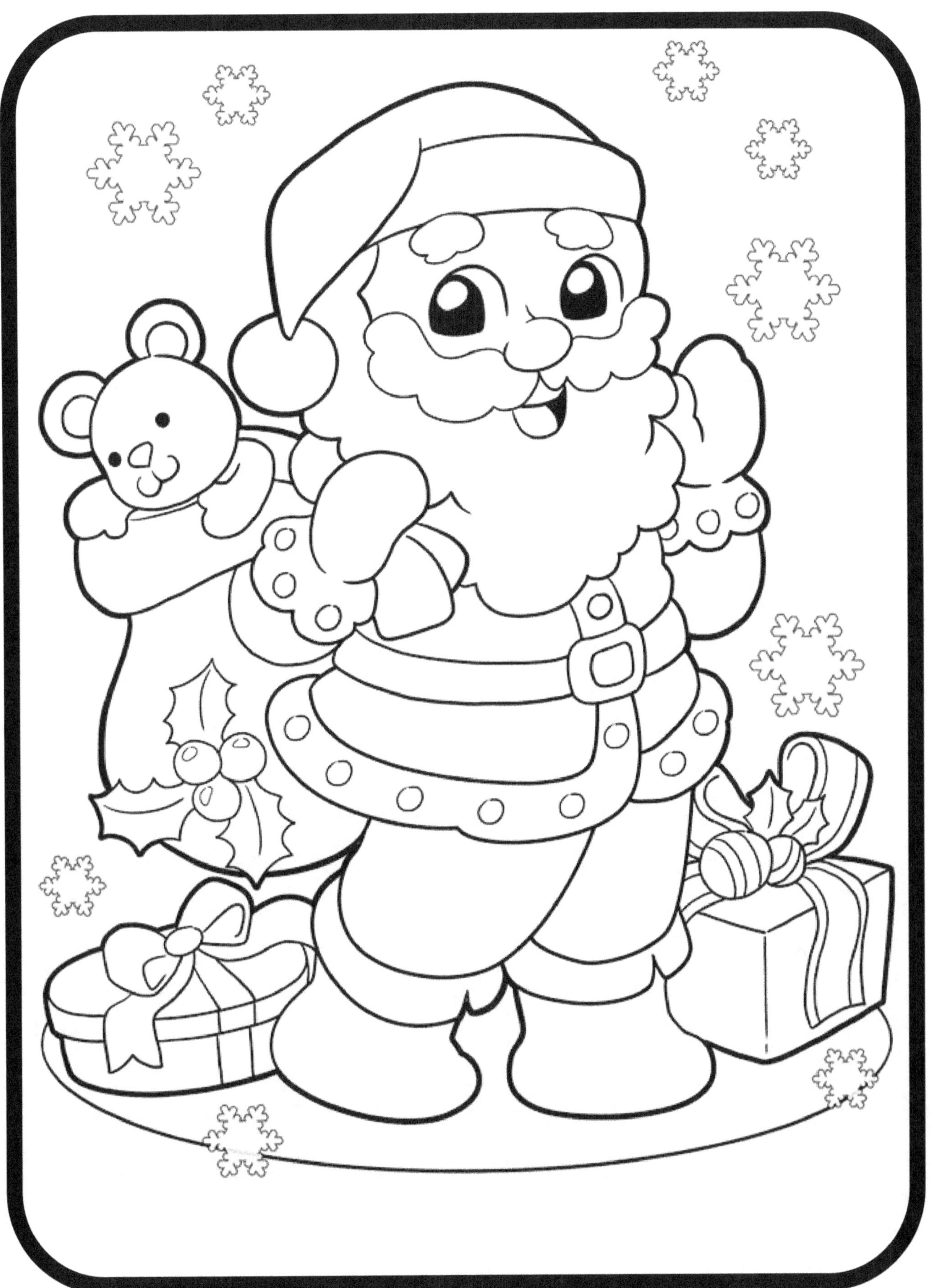

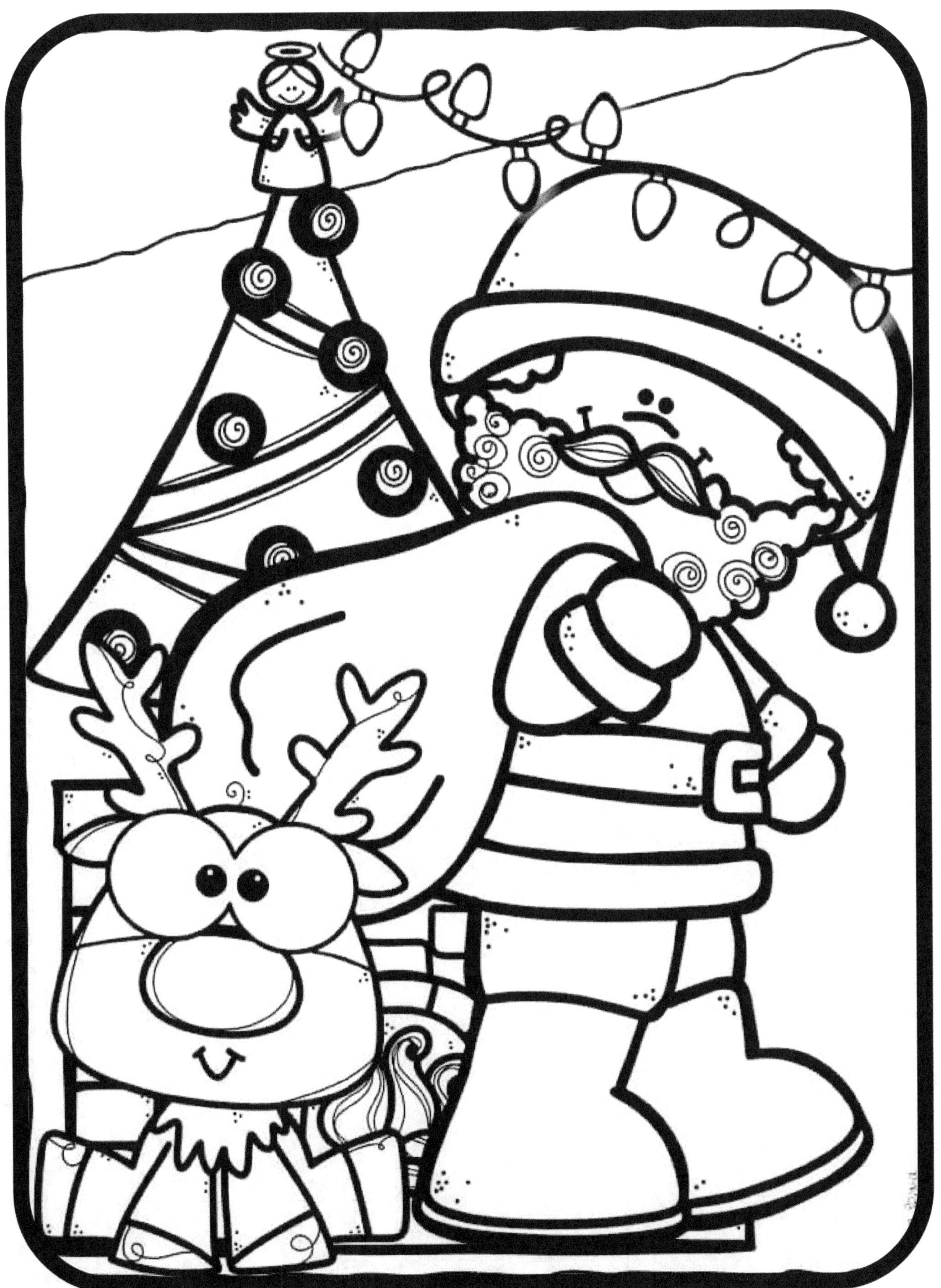

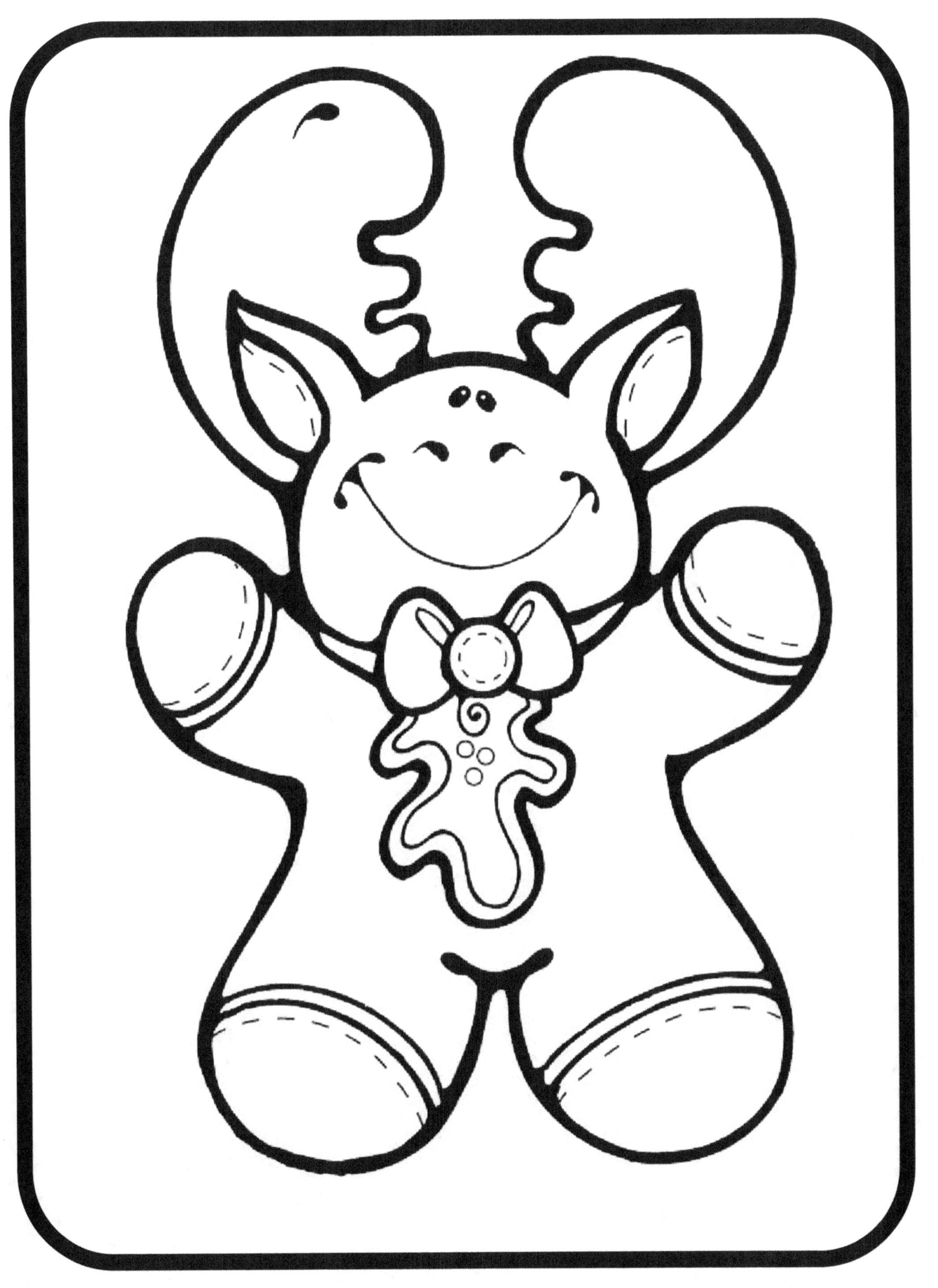

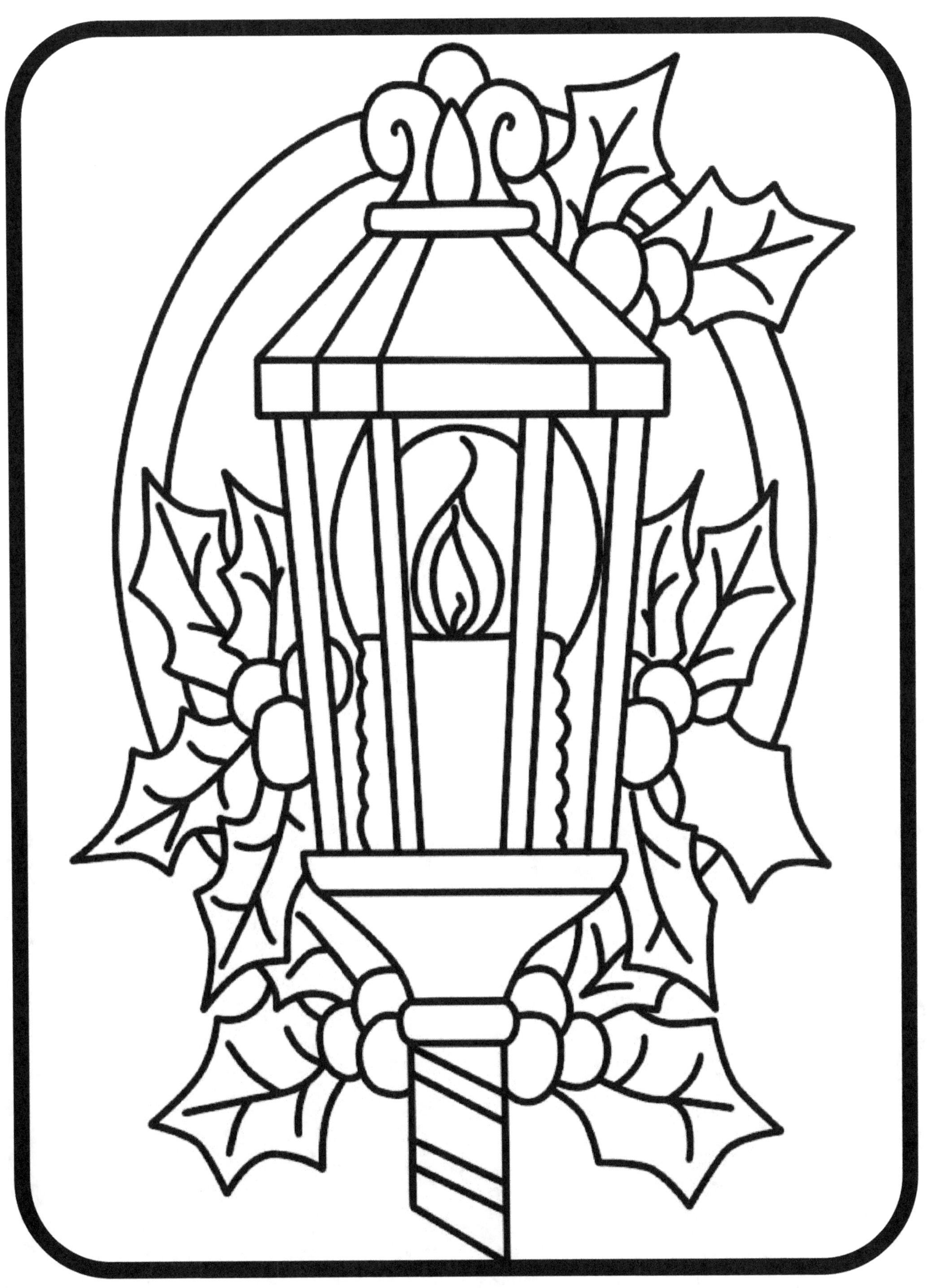

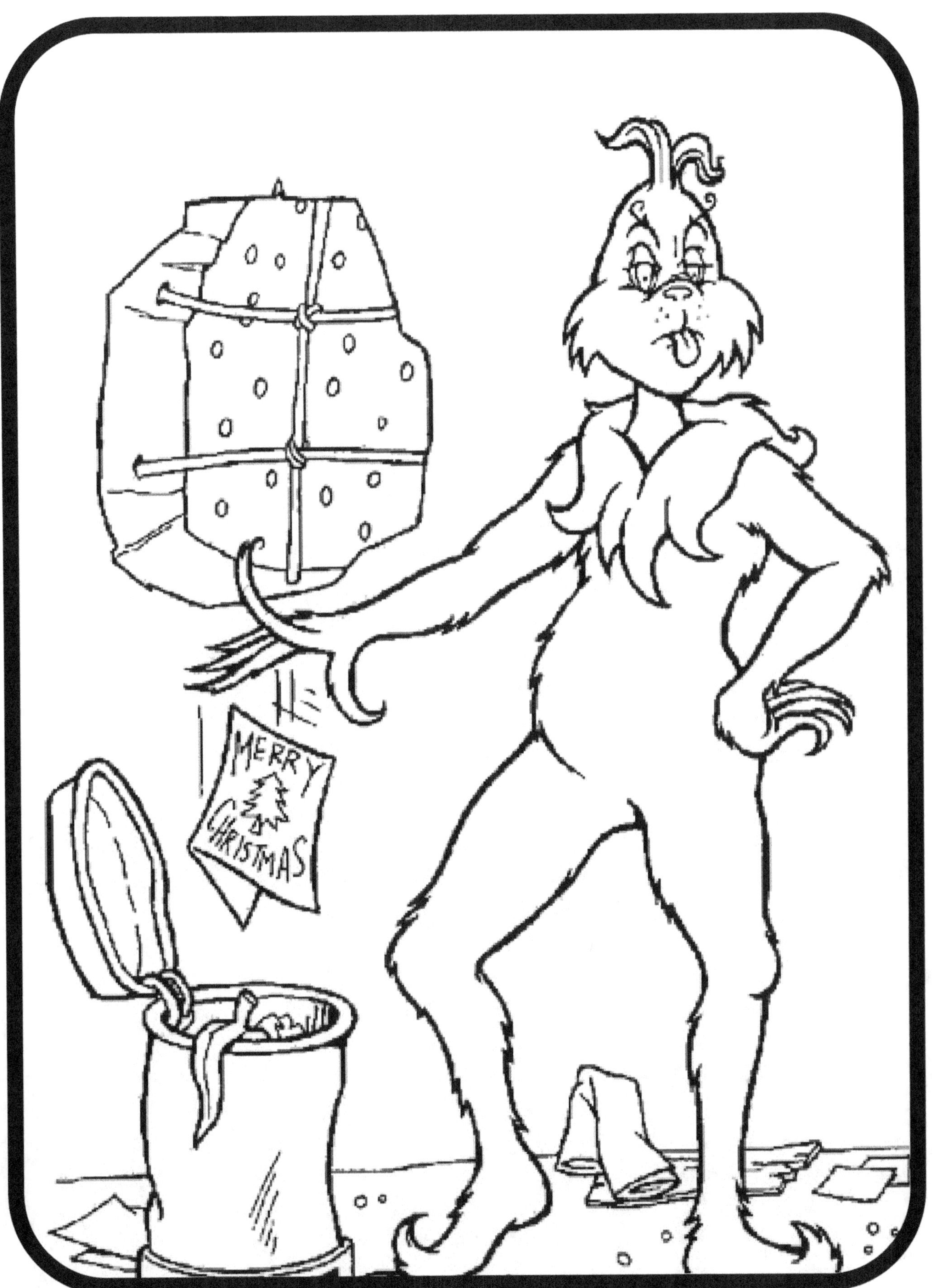

MERRY
CHRISTMAS

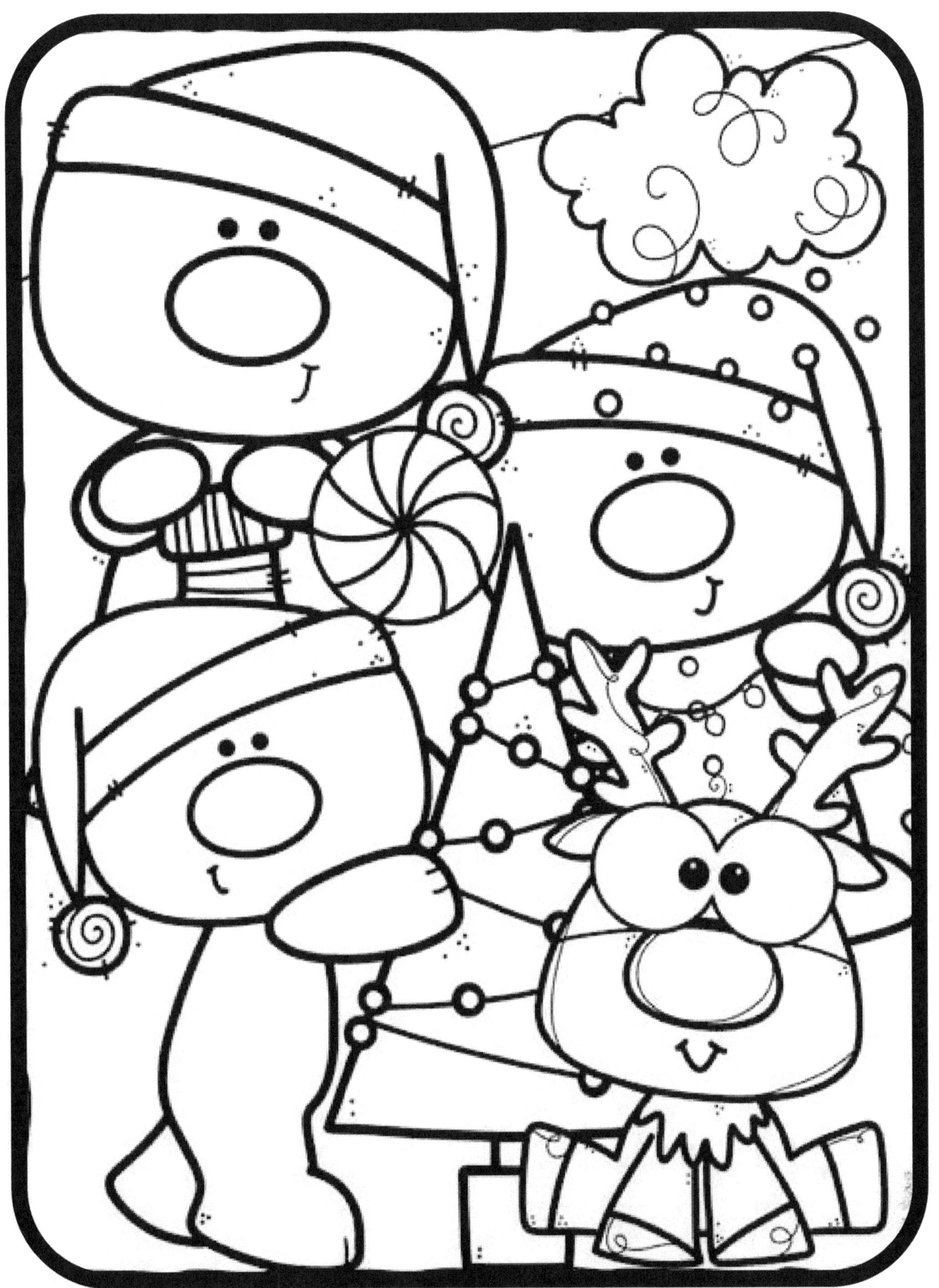

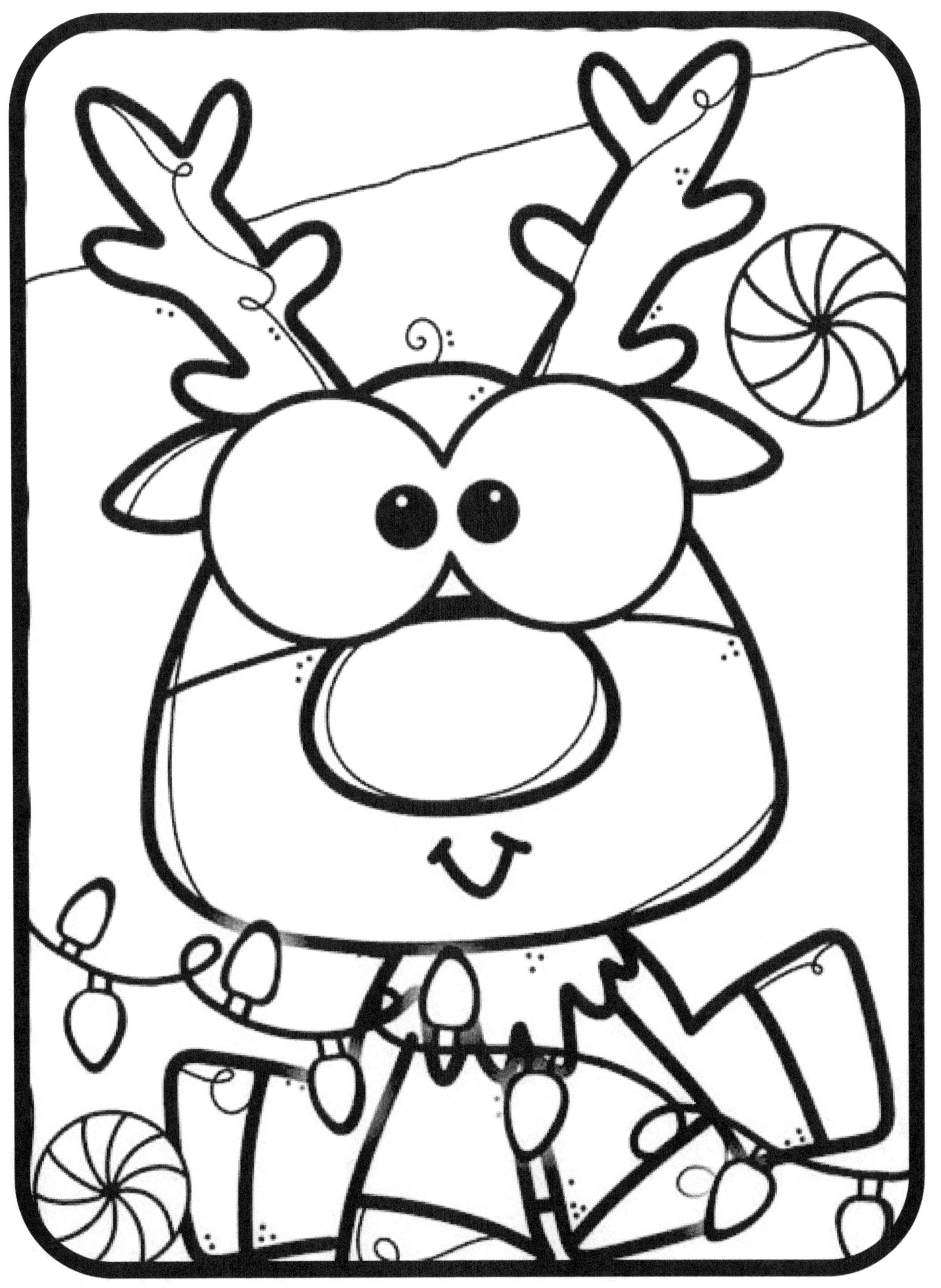

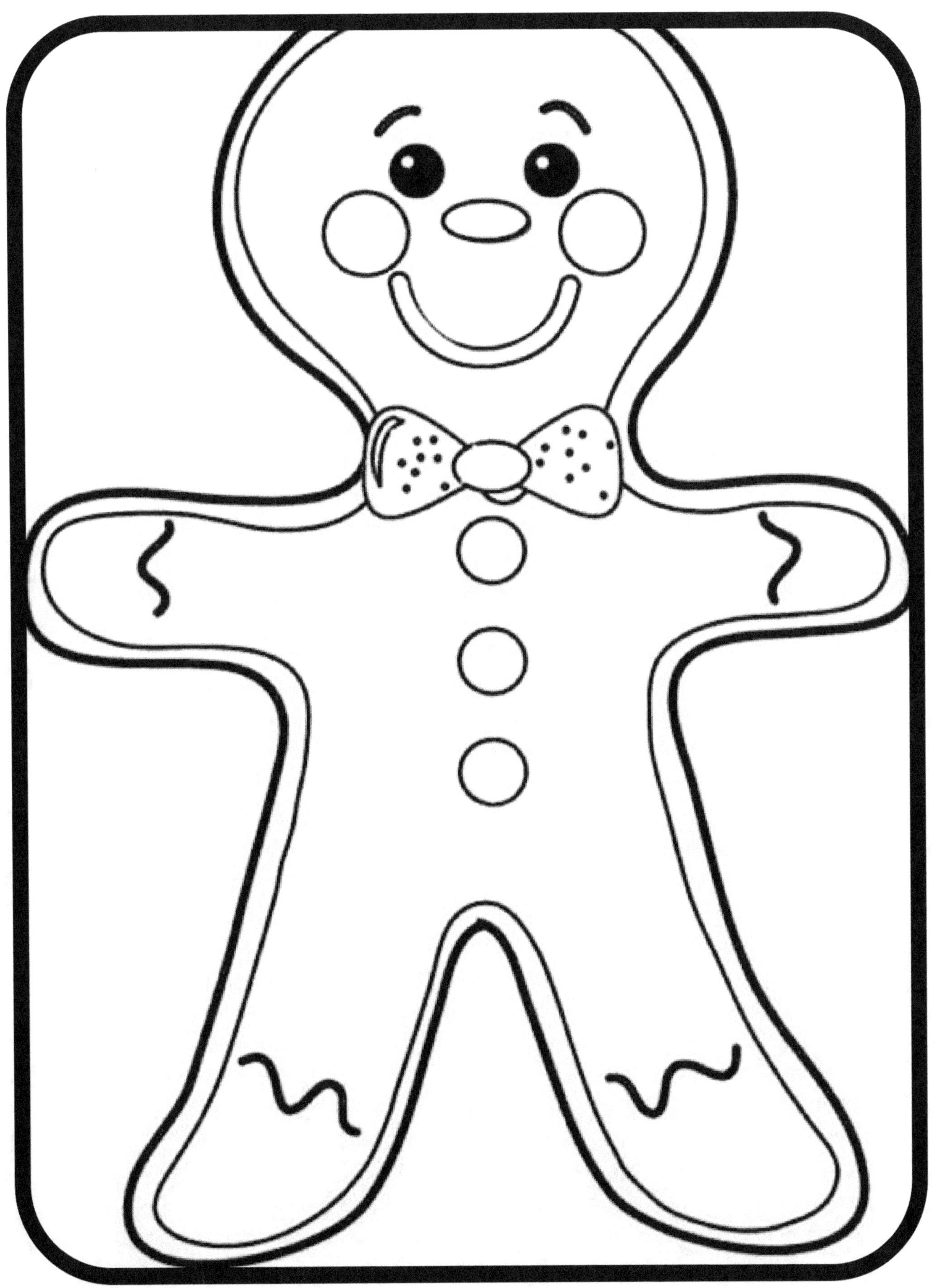

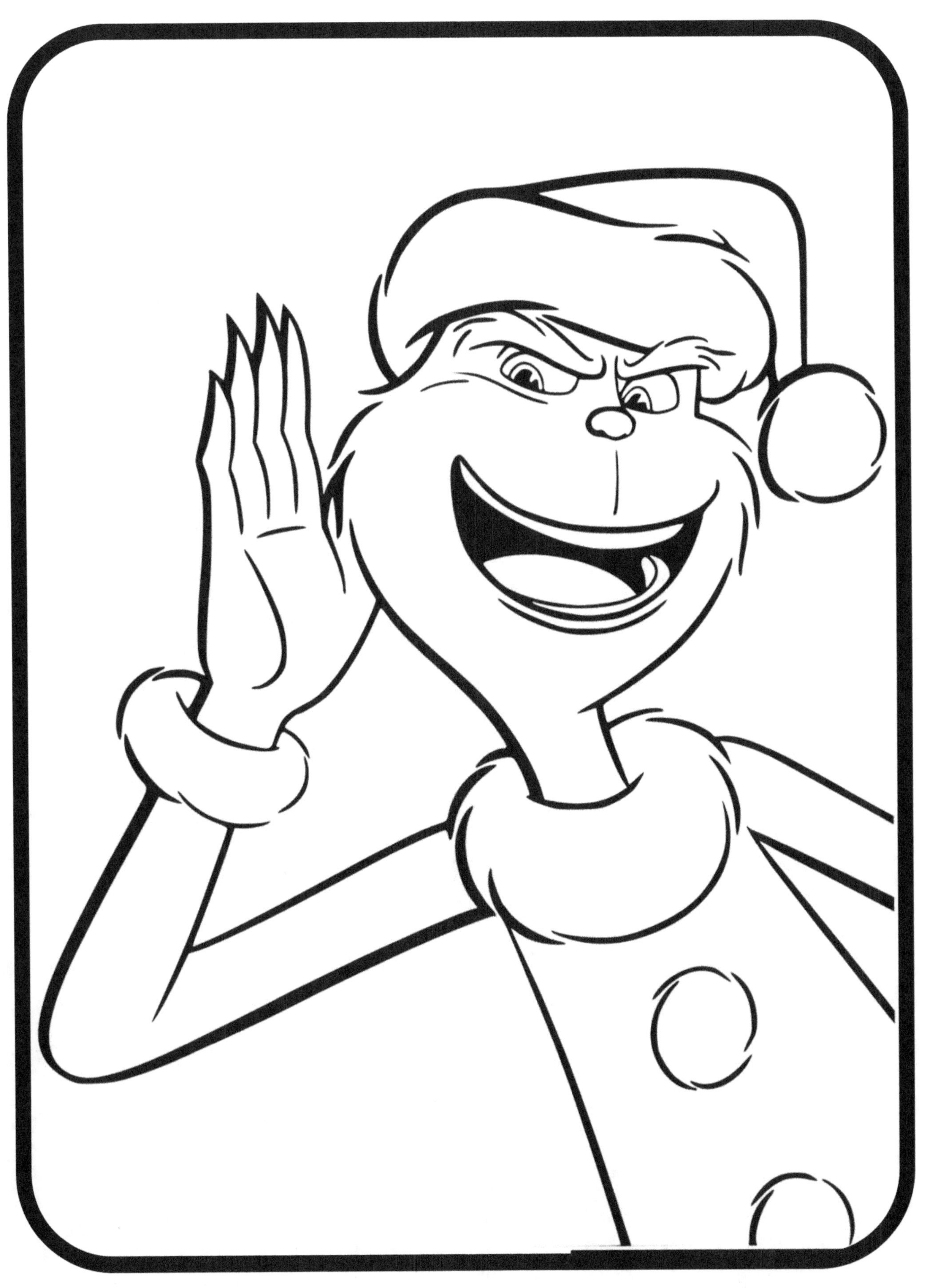

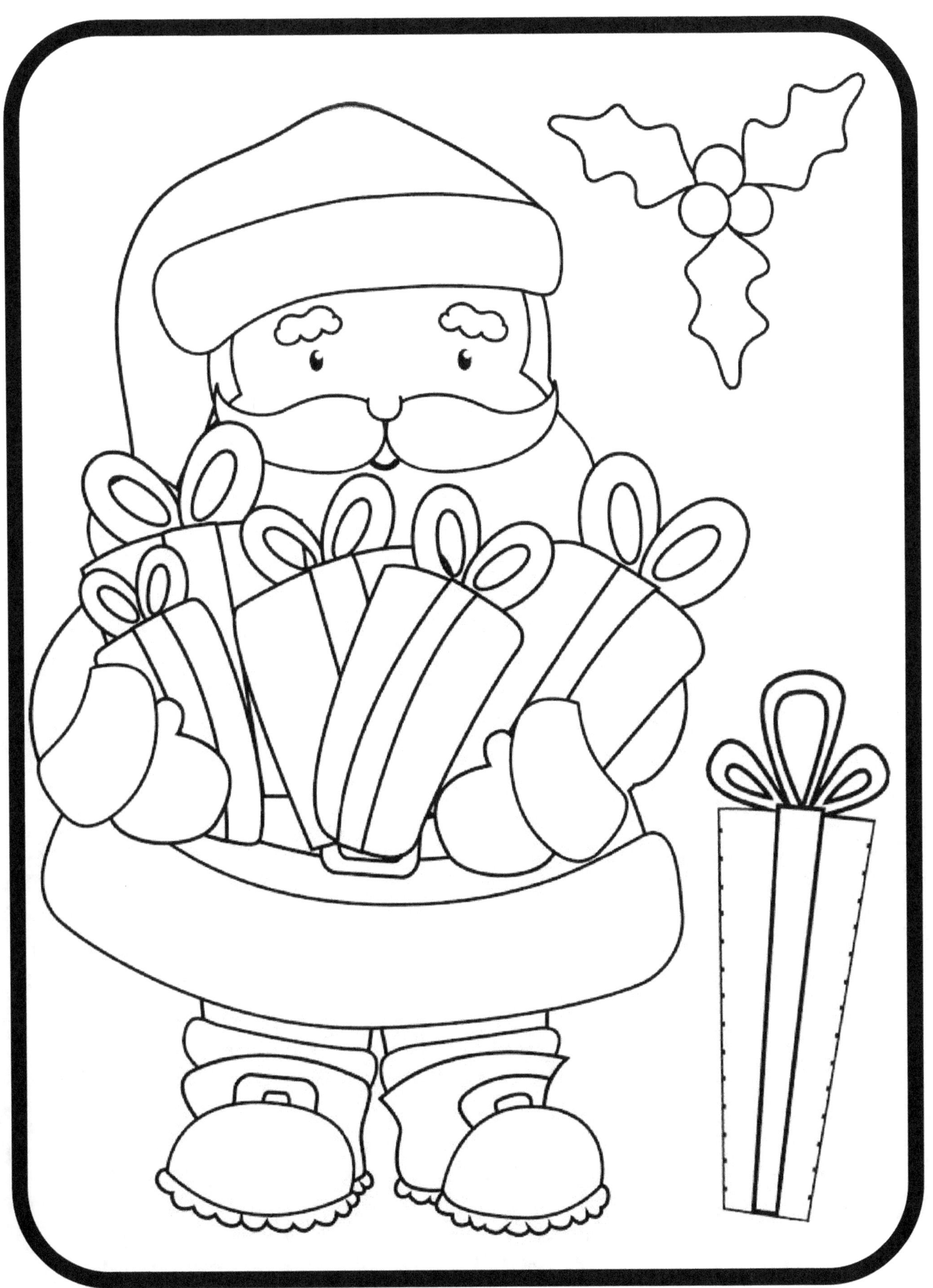

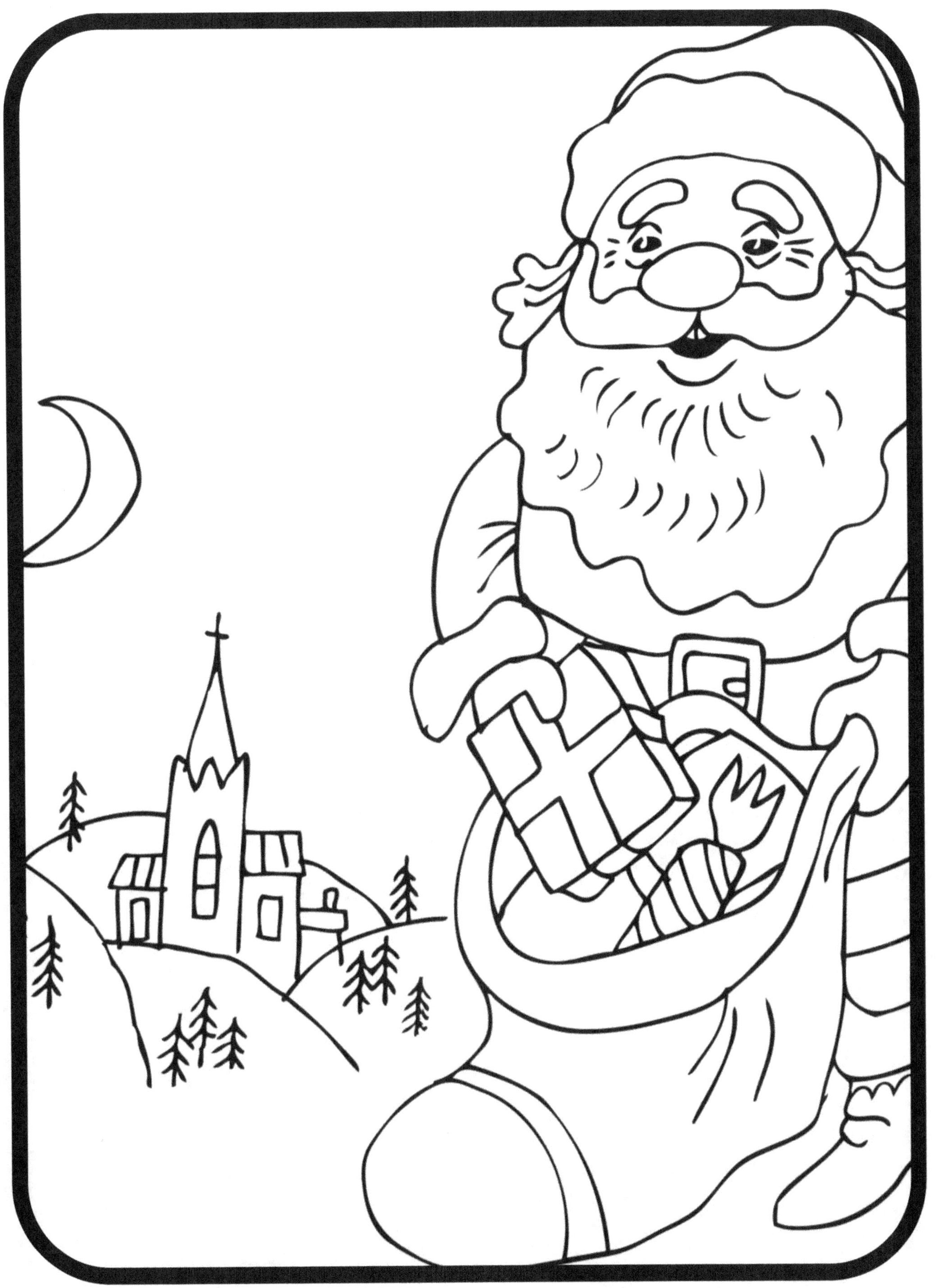

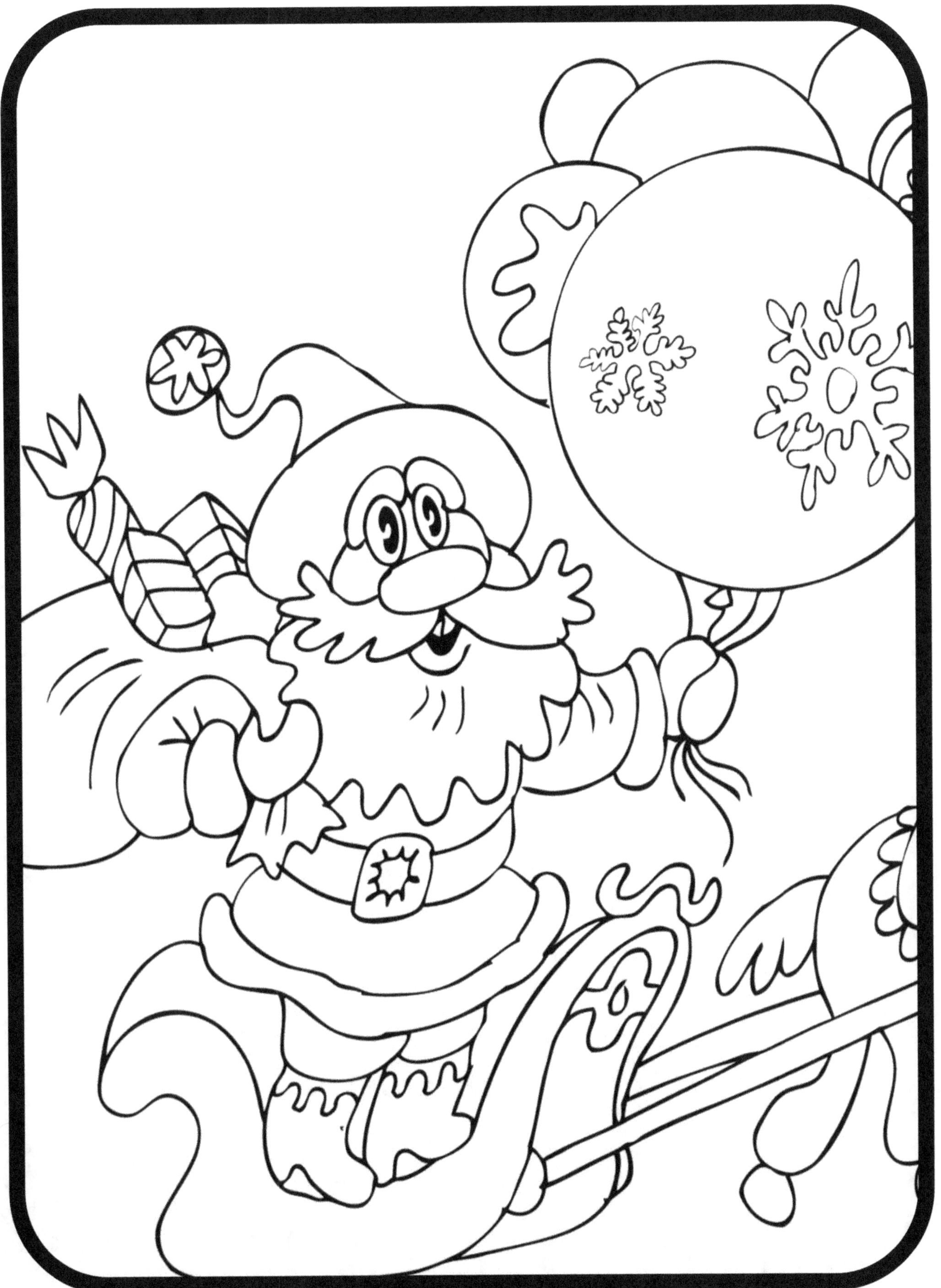

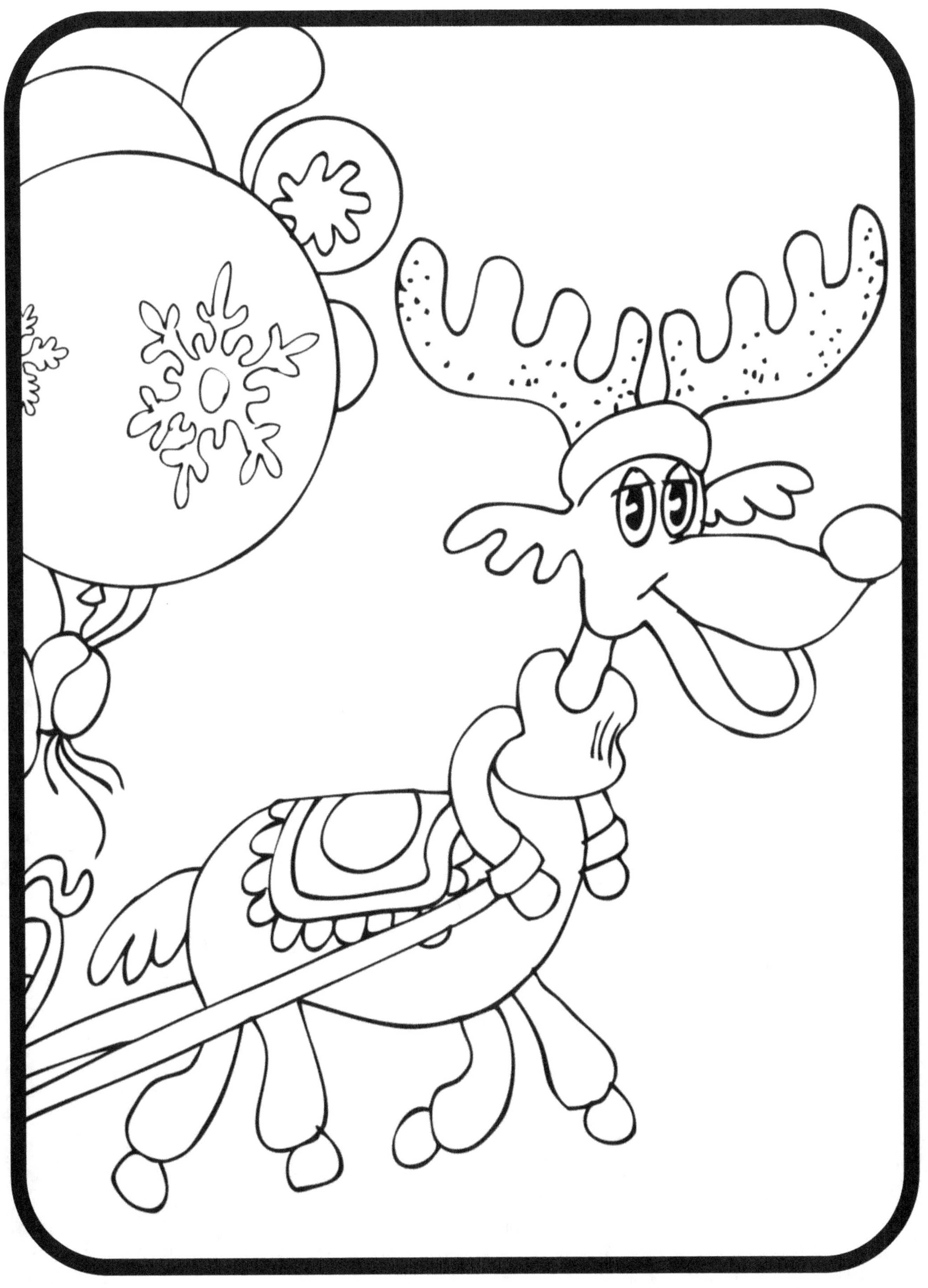

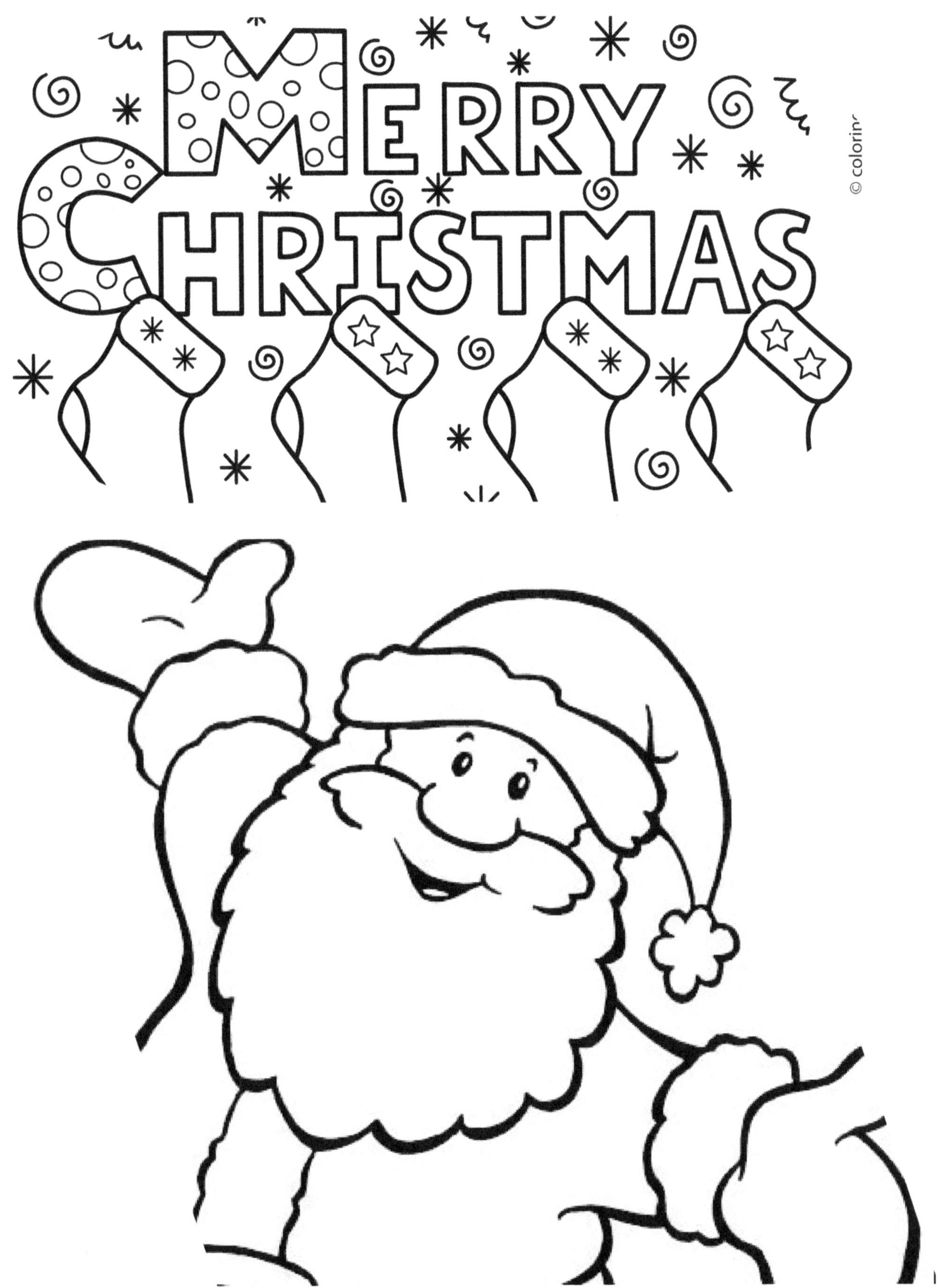

MERRY CHRISTMAS